Programming Microcomputers With PASCAL

Programming Microcomputers With PASCAL

M. D. Beer

Department of Computer Science University of Liverpool

VNR VAN NOSTRAND REINHOLD COMPANY

NEW YORK CINCINNATI TORONTO LONDON MELBOURNE

Library of Congress Catalog Card Number: 82-4863
ISBN: 0-442-21368-9

Printed in Great Britain

First published in Great Britain 1982 by Granada Publishing,
Frogmore, St. Albans, Herts AL2 2NF
and 36 Golden Square, London W1R 4AH

First published in U.S.A. 1982 by Van Nostrand Reinhold Company Inc.
135 West 50th Street, New York, N.Y. 10020
Reprinted 1983

Van Nostrand Reinhold Publishing
1410 Birchmount Road
Scarborough, Ontario M1P 2E7, Canada

Van Nostrand Reinhold Australia Pty. Ltd.
17 Queen Street
Mitcham, Victoria 3132, Australia

Van Nostrand Reinhold Company Limited
Molly Millars Lane
Wokingham, Bershire, England

15 14 13 12 11 10 9 8 7 6 5 4 3 2

Library of Congress Cataloging in Publication Data

Beer, Martin D.
Programming microcomputers with PASCAL.

Includes index.
1. PASCAL (Computer program language) 2. Microcomputers-Programming.
I. Title.
QA76.73.P2B44 001.64'24 82-4863
ISBN 0-442-21368-9 AACR2

Contents

Preface

PASCAL was originally developed as a teaching language for students of computer science. It has the elements of simplicity, and, at the same time, provides a wide range of data types and structures which can be used to very good effect. Until the coming of relatively cheap microcomputers, the use of computers was restricted to those people fortunate enough to be working for or studying in an organisation that owned one of these expensive machines, and was prepared to make a small amount of time available for programs to be written.

With the coming of the microcomputer all this has changed. It is now possible to purchase machines that will perform extremely complex tasks and store large volumes of information for very little more than the cost of an office electric typewriter. The problem is that once the machine is available, it must be told what it is expected to do. This requires the writing of a program. While most of the tasks that the microcomputer will perform will be perfectly adequately catered for by the purchase of packaged programs, the full potential of the microcomputer can only be realised if some programs can be written for it.

The great advantage of PASCAL is that it is possible to provide a full compiler, together with the filing system and text editor that make a complete programming environment, all within the constraints of the currently available microcomputers. A lot of work has also gone in to the development of portable compilers, themselves written in PASCAL, that can be transferred comparatively easily from computer to computer. It has therefore been possible to install PASCAL compilers on a very large number of computers, very rapidly. Another advantage of this approach has been that the language accepted by all the compilers was almost completely compatible, even though no official standard then existed (and, at the time of writing, still does not exist).

With the advent of microcomputers, further work has been done, notably by Professor Kenneth Bowles' team at the University of California, San Diego, to develop a complete program development system that is independent of the microcomputer on which it is run. This means that not only is the compiler the same but so is the file organisation, filing system, program editor and command monitor. Also the programmer is not tied to any one machine, but can use any system that supports UCSD PASCAL. As far as he is concerned, they all look the same, and his programs behave in exactly the same way. This is possible because the compiler does not generate code for any particular microprocessor, but a general intermediate code, called p-code. All that is then necessary to transfer the whole system to a new microprocessor is to write an interpreter to execute these P-codes, which is a far easier job than writing the complete compiler.

This book is intended to be an informal introduction to programming in PASCAL. The examples have been chosen to show how programs can be written that solve everyday problems, of the sort for which the availability of microcomputers has become most useful. Unlike most introductory programming text books intended for use by students studying computer science, this book discusses different aspects of programming in a functional way. The early chapters deal with the ways in which data is stored and manipulated. The different ways of controlling how a program operates and how it can be split into manageable portions then follows. It is very useful to be able to group items of data together when they have a valid association, such as a series of data points, or all the information known about some object. PASCAL has a wide variety of different constructs that allow the programmer to structure his data in the most appropriate way for the problem under consideration. The storage of data in files often gives newcomers some problems so it is discussed in some detail.

The elements of good programming are stressed in many places throughout the book. It has been thought necessary, however, to include two chapters on programming practices, one on structured programming at the beginning, and one on top-down design at the end. It is essential to break long programs into manageable segments that can be worked on in comfort. If this is done in a sensible way, each segment having a definite task, the work required to obtain a working program can be greatly diminished. The last chapter looks at some of the special problems encountered with programming control systems that have to interact with the outside world. As microcomputers become cheaper this is becoming a very important aspect of their use. Traditionally, most of these programs have been written in assembler, but for a long time it has been realised that the use of a high-level language, such as PASCAL, would be a great aid. Several languages have been designed for just this purpose. But why go to all the bother of learning yet another language, and all its conventions, when a suitable general-purpose language, such as PASCAL, can be used instead?

It is very important, that in a book such as this the programming examples should be checked very carefully. There is, in practice, no better way of doing this than to run them on a suitable computer. All the programs in this book were therefore written and checked on an APPLE II microcomputer, running the latest version of APPLE PASCAL. Because of inconsistencies in UCSD PASCAL, on which the APPLE version is based with other common versions, some post-editing has been necessary. Most programs should run with little or no alteration on any reasonably standard PASCAL compiler. The only area where there may be problems, is in the file handling, where the accepted PASCAL standard is very deficient for the microcomputer operating environment. The APPLE file opening and closing procedures used when writing these programs are therefore given in Appendix B, and can be used, either directly, if the program is to be run under UCSD PASCAL, or suitable routines can be written, when similar provision is provided under different operating systems.

Finally, I would like to thank all my friends and collegues, whose helpful comments have made this book possible. I would particularily like to thank Professor J. L. Alty, Director of the Computer Laboratory, University of Liverpool for the use of the various microcomputers to prepare both the programs and the manuscript of this book.

Martin D. Beer

CHAPTER 1

Programming Microcomputer Systems

1.1 INTRODUCTION

The coming of cheap microcomputer systems has opened up a new world to many professional scientists and engineers. The power of the computer is no longer locked away within a special air-conditioned machine room, tended by hoards of professional computer operators and programmers who have little interest in running what are often comparatively small engineering programs and disrupting their tidy schedules. It is now possible to buy a reasonably-configured microcomputer system with a keyboard and display, adequate storage capacity for both programs and data, and a small printer for permanent hard-copy output, for less than £1000. If better storage or printing facilities are required, for instance, for the production of output suitable for inclusion directly within technical and management reports, these can be bought at a little extra expense. In addition, a whole range of other peripherals can be added to the system, some traditionally associated with computers, such as digital plotters, but also many new ones, including such things as speech recognition and synthesis units, which allow the microcomputer to perform tasks that are totally impossible with larger machines.

The capital cost of the microcomputer is now so low that it is possible to install one in the office, workshop or laboratory exactly where access to computer power is most needed. In addition it is also practical to connect the microcomputer directly to any test equipment being used so that it can collect the data which it will later be required to analyse and store itself. Many routine tests can be automated further, with the microcomputer controlling at least the routine part of the procedure directly, so that the operator only needs to set up the equipment, answer a series of questions about the test procedure to be used before leaving the microcomputer to supervise the rest of the test sequence.

In most cases the microcomputer will be bought and maintained directly by the office, workshop or laboratory from its own funds, without reference to a specialist computing department, and without the longer term support that such an organisation can be expected to provide.

Buying a microcomputer is only the first stage. Before it can be used, it must be told exactly what it is to do. This is done by providing it with a program, or sequence of instructions, that it can execute, which will eventually result in it achieving the desired goal. Since programs form such an important part of all computer systems, they are known collectively by a special name, software, which differentiates them from the actual physical electronics of the machine known as hardware.

Even to perform the simplest of tasks, a number of programs will be needed. Some will be provided by the microcomputer manufacturer, either as part of the machine package or as optional extras. Typically these will include everything that is needed to program the machine in BASIC (a simple calculator-like language), various housekeeping utilities to make the machine usable, programs to allow for the maintainance of files on floppy diskettes, etc., and a number of demonstration programs that show the advantages of the particular machine to the best advantage. None of these programs is likely to tackle the problem that the microcomputer is intended to solve. To do this other programs must be obtained. This may be done in a number of different ways:

(a) By purchasing a suitable program, or software package, that has been developed for a very large market. Since development costs are spread over a large number of end-users, highly sophisticated programs can be obtained very cheaply. However the cost of packaging, marketing and distribution must also be covered, so programs must be written in such a way that they will appeal to the largest possible community.

(b) Paying someone to write the programs required. This is very expensive as all the programming cost must be borne by this one program, which is likely never to be sold again. It may, however, be worthwhile if the microcomputer is to solve a particular problem, and the cost savings justify it.

(c) The end-user can write the programs himself. This is the most likely final solution. Even if a software package is initially selected, or an independent programmer is paid to write the first suite of programs, other jobs will be found for the microcomputer, or the job specification will change, which will make it necessary to modify the existing programs.

As can be seen, buying programs, either in the form of packages, or having them specifically written only provides part of the answer. To ensure that the final result does exactly what is required, it is usually much faster, and almost always easier if the programs are written by the person who originally specified them. To this end almost all the popular microcomputer systems provide software with which to develop programs. This is usually in terms of BASIC. BASIC is chosen because it is easy to learn, and because the machine resources needed to run programs written in it are not very extravagant. This allows it to be implemented successfully on all but the smallest microcomputer systems. BASIC does, however, have a number of distinct disadvantages for the serious programmer. These only become apparent as programs become longer and more complex. This book describes another programming language which has become very popular with microcomputer programmers. This language, called PASCAL, was designed by Professor Nicklaus Wirth of E.T.H. Zurich in the late 1960s, initially to teach his students how to program.

Chapter 2 discusses how programs are designed, and the building blocks that are used to construct them. The next five chapters describe how these features are implemented in PASCAL. Since PASCAL was originally designed as a teaching language, these ideas were included as an integral part of the language.

While the design of the program is very important, it is only useful if it can act sensibly on the data that it is intended to process. This can only be done if the data can be arranged in a way that best represents the information to be stored. Chapters 8 to 12 are concerned with the organisation of items of related data, in ways that they can best be processed.

The final chapter discusses some of the peculiar problems involved when programs have to interact with external devices.

1.2 THE ELEMENTS OF A MICROCOMPUTER SYSTEM

Before examining the construction of programs further, it is necessary to consider the different components that go together to make up a complete microcomputer system, as seen from the programmer's point of view. Figure 1.1 shows these units, and how they are connected together to make a usable system. The user communicates with the microcomputer through the input unit and some sort of output unit. The input unit is usually a typewriter-type keyboard and the output unit a video display, but it may well be a printer, which would enable a permanent record to be kept. There may also also be additional subsidiary input and output devices which can be used in place of the main units, or can be controlled by user programs.

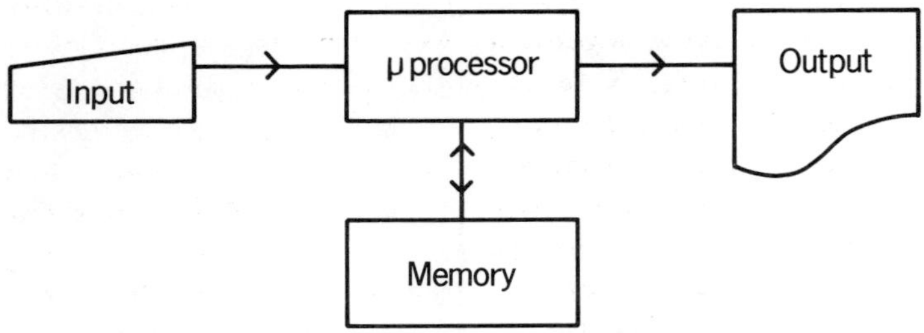

Figure 1.1 The basics of a simple microcomputer system

As has already been seen, all computers are controlled by sequences of commands which are held within its memory. These sequences of commands, called programs, tell the computer, which is by its nature a general-purpose device, exactly what it is to do. The repertoire of instructions is designed so that all the basic operations likely to be needed in any computer program can be performed. The actual operations which are called for in the program are executed in the central component of the microcomputer, the microprocessor. The essential difference between a microcomputer system and any other computer system is that the central processor of the microcomputer system is a single microelectronic component, costing less than £5, whereas in mainframe and mini-computers the heart of the system consists of specially designed logic occupying several printed circuit boards, and therefore costing considerably more.

The total memory available within the microcomputer can be further sub-divided into a relatively small amount of main storage, all the contents of which are immediately available to the microcomputer, and a much larger amount of backing storage, which is not. The main memory consists of read-only memory, the contents of which the microprocessor can read, but not change, and read-write memory that the microprocessor can change at will. The advantage of read-only memory, however, is that, unlike most forms of read-write memory, its contents are not lost when the power is turned off. This makes read-only memory eminently suitable for the storage of programs and data which are always required, such as those provided by the microcomputer manufacturer to take over control of the machine as soon as the power is switched on, and to control the interfaces to various input and output devices, the detailed operation of which is of little interest to the user so long as a simple standard interface to his program is provided.

Read-write memory is used to store transient programs and data that are loaded, as required, from the backing storage available. For a program which is being developed, care must be taken to store it on backing storage before it is either overwritten by the next program or lost when the power is turned off. Early microcomputers used standard audio cassette recorders, because both the recorders and the cassette tapes themselves are cheap and readily available. In computer terms, however, the speed that data can be written and read back by this method is very slow, and it is often very difficult to find the information required on a very long tape because the right section of tape must be positioned under the tape head.

Figure 1.2 shows how all of these units may be connected together to make a small microcomputer system.

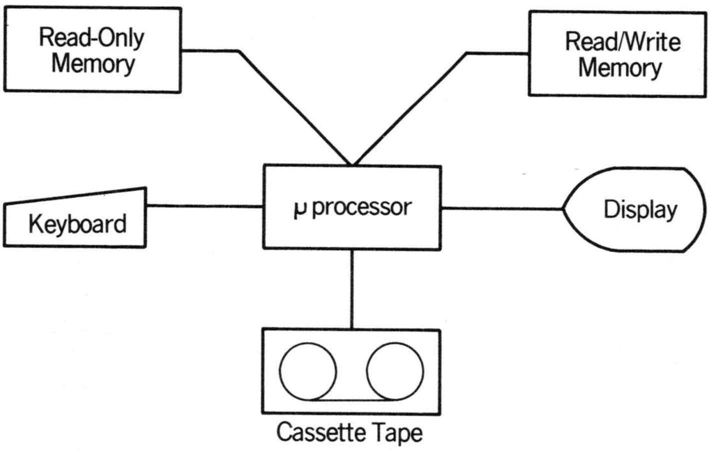

Figure 1.2 The memory and backing store likely to be found on a small microcomputer system

It is now becoming much more common to use floppy diskettes as the main backing storage on microcomputers. They have a number of distinct advantages, in that data can be transferred to and from the main memory much more rapidly, and different programs, and sets of data, can be accessed without difficulty, so long as the right diskette is inserted into the drive. Figure 1.3 shows a fully configured microcomputer system with floppy diskette drives and a printer.

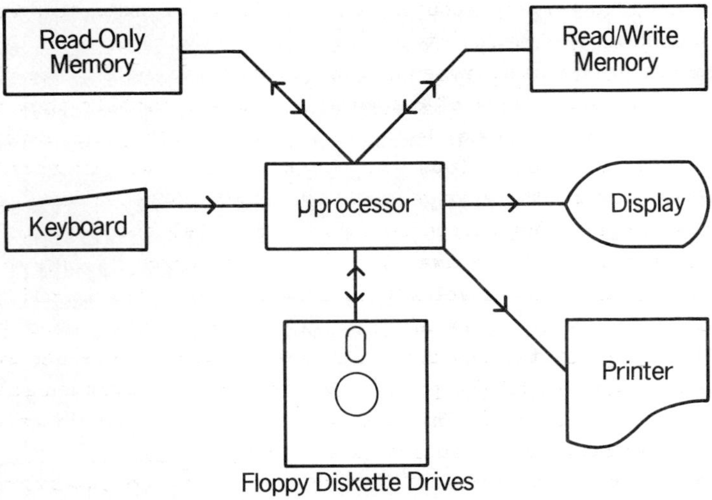

Figure 1.3 The facilities likely to be available on a fully configured microcomputer system

Between the microcomputer and the external devices to which it is connected, some special circuitry, known as an interface, is required to convert the electronic signals sent out by the microprocessor into meaningful commands for the external unit, and the data coming in to the right form for it to be accepted by the microprocessor. In addition to converting the data, the interface can tell the microprocessor a certain amount of useful information about itself, such as whether there is data to be collected, or whether it is ready to accept more. This information is essential if the data is not to be lost, either because it is being sent more rapidly than the device can accept it, or the microcomputer is ready to receive more data before the interface has it available. It is necessary for the programmer to manage these signals in special routines, called drivers. For most common micromputers, these drivers are provided as part of the systems software, and all that is needed is to plug in the required peripheral, and turn the machine on. It is only when it is intended to connect the microcomputer to non-standard peripherals that they need to be written by the user.

1.3 DEVELOPING A PROGRAM USING A COMPILER

Before a program can be executed, it must first be converted from the computer language in which it is written, into machine code that the microprocessor can understand, and then stored in the computer's memory. In the early days of computing, this was usually done by the programmer, on paper. It is, however, a time consuming and repetitive job that requires meticulous attention to the smallest detail. In other words, it is the sort of task for which computers are ideally suited. It was not long before programs were developed that took some of the more routine tasks away from the programmer. This, in turn, allowed programs being developed to become more complex, and slowly much of the pure drudgery of programming was taken over by the computer itself. Initially, programs were translated one instruction at a time, each line of the program source being converted into one machine code instruction. This was very useful, in that it saved the programmer a considerable amount of book-keeping.

Over the years two distinct ways of developing computer programs have arisen. In each, the basic aim is the same, to convert the source text of the program into instructions that the computer can understand, in other words, machine code. The way each operates, is however, very different.

The first high-level languages that were installed on microcomputer systems, notably BASIC, were interpreted. An interpreter works by reading each line of the source text which is stored in the microcomputer's memory, and executing it directly. By this method each line is executed in turn. It is usual to provide, at least, an elementary program editor which allows the programmer to enter and change the program held in memory, and special instructions to store the program on some form of backing store, and return it to memory when required, as part of the interpreter package. Since backing store is only required for the permanent storage of programs, a slow, but cheap, form of backing storage, such as cassette tape, is all that is required. This is particularly so if the interpreter, and other necessary system software, is held permanently in read-only memory within the microcomputer itself. Figure 1.4 shows how a user would view a typical interpreter.

Compilers, on the other hand, work by translating the whole of the program into the microcomputer's machine code, and storing it on backing storage so that it may later be loaded into memory and executed directly. Since the source code is only translated once, rather than every time it is to be executed, as is the case with an interpreter, the code generated by a compiler will generally execute much more rapidly than if the program was executed using an

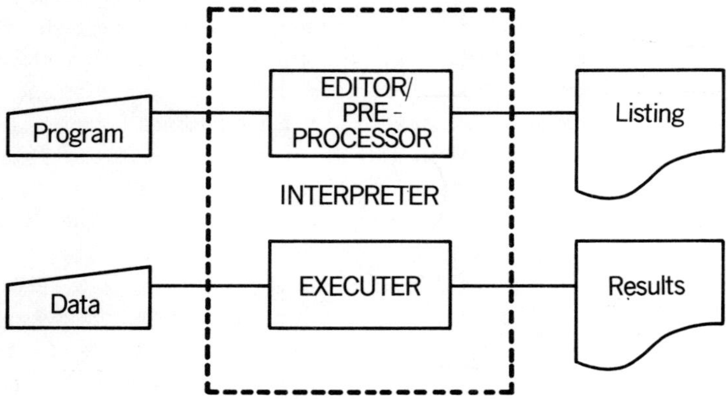

Figure 1.4 Developing a program using an interpreter

interpreter. A compiler has to do much more work, however, to translate the program completely into machine code, and therefore the compiler generally requires considerably more memory space than an interpreter for a similar language. Also, it is far more difficult to find out exactly what has happened before an error is reported when the program has been compiled because all the information held in the source text is no longer available to the error handling system. This makes manipulation of the source text much more important, and therefore quite sophisticated text editors have been developed to assist the programmer in writing his program. Figure 1.5 shows the stages that must be gone through when compiling a program.

These are quite large programs in their own right, and there are very few systems that have enough memory available to allow both the text editor and the compiler to reside in memory at the same time, and allow sufficient space to develop worthwhile programs. Some form of backing store is therefore required, so that both the text editor and the compiler can be loaded into read/write memory rapidly when they are needed, as well as providing a convenient storage medium for both the source text of the program, entered through the text editor, and the machine codes generated by the compiler from it. This storage is usually provided in the form of floppy diskette drives attached to the microcomputer system. Figure 1.6 shows some of the programs that make up a typical development system, and how they relate to each other.

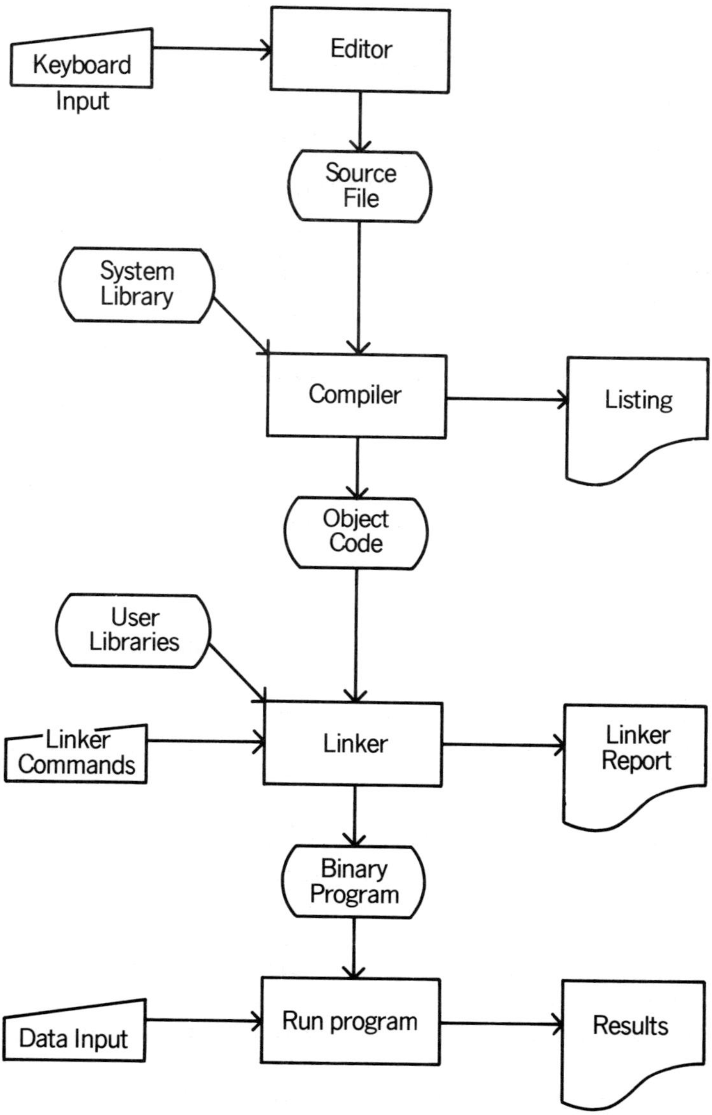

Figure 1.5 The stages in developing a program using a compiler

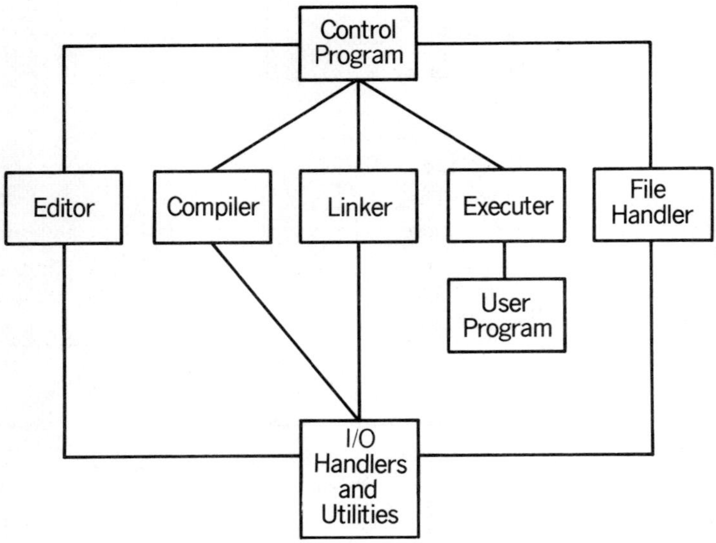

Figure 1.6 The parts of the available system software which make up a complete PASCAL system

1.4 PROBLEMS

1.1 If you own, or have access to a microcomputer system, read the documentation supplied, and identify the main parts:

(a) the microprocessor
(b) the main memory
(c) the backing store
(d) the input and output units attached.

If you can, find out how much read-only, and read-write memory is available for your use, and what programs, if any, are stored in read-only memory.

1.2 Use the text editor provided within your PASCAL system to enter the following program:

```
PROGRAM first(input,output);

BEGIN
    writeln('this is my first PASCAL program')
END.
```

You will have to find the section of the manual for your PASCAL system which describes the text editor provided and follow the instructions on how to insert text, and amend it, if necessary, to store in memory what is written above, exactly. It must then be stored on disk, so that it is ready for the compiler to convert it into binary object code.

CHAPTER 2
Writing Programs

2.1 BEFORE YOU BEGIN

When starting to write a program, in the same way as with many other complex tasks, a certain amount of preparatory work is required. It is all too easy to start writing code immediately you have thought of some new idea. This is very rarely the best way to write a program, because, at this stage, you do not have a clear idea of what the program is intended to achieve. Until this is clear, it is effectively impossible to determine what is the best computational strategy to follow when writing the code. It is therefore necessary to do some preliminary work to ensure that the program that you are about to write will perform the task for which it is intended. Not only must its function be considered very carefully, but so also must the way in which it is to be used and whether it will interact with other parts of the microcomputer system, including the hardware, the operating system or other programs that are already in use.

It is impossible even to think of starting work on a program until some questions are settled, otherwise a great deal of work would be wasted. It is very easy to see the methodology of writing programs in terms of big computer systems and large programming teams. The small computer user writing his own programs faces exactly the same problems however, and does not have the same resources to overcome them. Only by a clear understanding of the problem that he wishes to solve, and a clear method of attack, can he hope to get the most out of both his time and the often somewhat limited computing resources available to him.

First of all, the answers to a number of questions must be known:

> A clear idea must be had of what the program is intended to achieve.

The input to be processed must be known, and the information that will be required in reports, output files for further processing, etc.

Also a clear idea must be had of the general algorithm, or problem solving strategy, to be used.

Only then is it possible to see whether or not the use of a computer is the best way of solving the problem. If, after fully analysing the problem, another way of solving it is found that does not require the use of a computer, then the most appropriate method should be used. The analysis work has not been a waste of time since the problem has been satisfactorily solved. Only then, is it possible to start work on the writing of the program.

2.2 WAYS OF DEVELOPING PROGRAMS

Once it has been decided that the best course of action is to use the

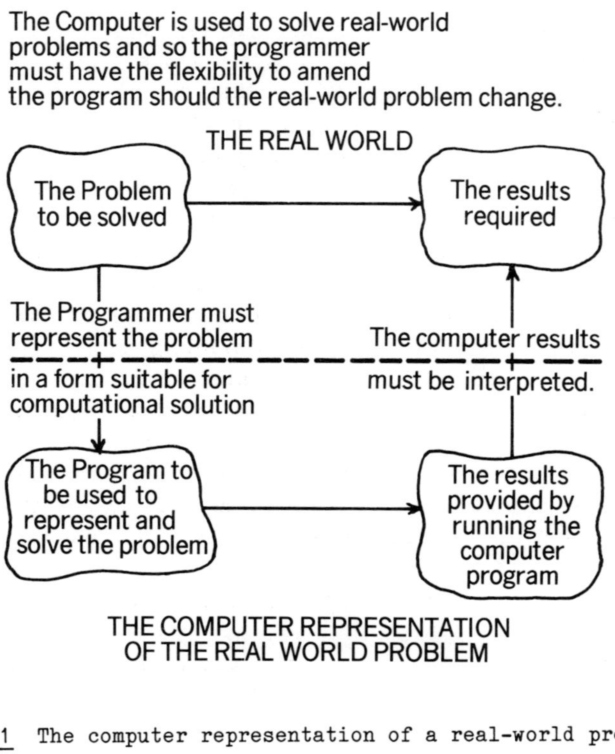

Figure 2.1 The computer representation of a real-world problem

computer, consideration must be given to how the program is to be written. This, of course, has been a problem since the earliest days of computers, and in the past a number of different strategies have been employed.

The object, as figure 2.1 shows, is to represent the problem, as perceived in the real world, as a computer program, which can be used to manipulate known data to give results that can be interpreted in terms of the real-world problem. If, say, an engineer wishes to discover whether a bridge is likely to collapse under some load, he could carry out the experiment, loading the bridge until it collapses. This would normally be considered a little bit dangerous unless some tests had been carried out first. What he might do is write a program which calculates the strains within the structure for a given load, by some mathematical model. He can then feed in the load he wishes to test, and an analysis of the results will tell him if the bridge is still standing or not. In this way the computed results may be related back to the problem in the real world.

Over the years many methods of analysing and writing programs have been used. Not all have been as successful as others, nor as widely used. Some of the more popular include:

> Coding from the start of the program, line-by-line. This is the way that beginners usually attempt to write a program. It works, so long as the total program is very short and does not contain long or complicated loops. Unfortunately, the statements in very few programs are executed in exactly the order they are written. It will be seen in many examples in this book how the execution path through a program can vary greatly, depending on the form and amount of input data. In addition, no account is taken of the most important parts of the program. These are the sections of code that control the whole action of the program, or are to be executed most often. It is very tempting to spend a lot of time on the first few lines, but to hurriedly put together the rest which might be executed many hundreds of times.
>
> A very large number of programmers start somewhere in the middle of the program, usually at the point that they think they know best, and work outwards from there. After deciding on the general solution, a rough sketch of the final program is produced, often containing specific code for the 'important' parts. Since initialisation is often considered 'unimportant', this part of the program is often left to later. It is hoped that the code already written will not require drastic revision

before the final version is obtained. A complete program can then be written, and revised again and again, until a satisfactory version emerges. The revisions often include drastic rewrites, and so considerable effort is wasted on coding that will never appear in the final program. Also no special thought is given to the most important parts of the program on which it all depends.

Some programmers spend a considerable time analysing the 'flow of control', producing detailed flow charts etc. to show exactly how the program will generate its final result. This is a method which has been used effectively for many years to produce the large program suites which are in use every day on large computers. The overall flow chart is used to break down the problem into a number of modules which are then tackled individually. Once all the modules have been written, they are put together, and the interfaces are firmed up so that the complete system functions satisfactorily. The problem is that the program is designed around the order in which the program is executed, rather than its basic structure, which may well not be understood properly. Also subsidiary modules may well be partially written before their interfaces, and therefore their complete function, has been finalised.

The 'bottom-up' approach still has some adherents, particularly amongst assembler-level programmers who are intimately involved with the hardware of their machines. Here, the lowest levels of the program are written first, and the programmer works steadily to higher levels until a complete program emerges. Despite its attractions to the programmer who feels seriously constrained by the underlying hardware of the computer, this approach suffers from a number of serious defects. Specific decisions, about how particular sections of the program are to be coded, must be made before the complete structure has been finalised. Notably, the interface between different modules is defined when that module is written, before the higher level, which will use it, has been designed. If an error is made, which only comes to light when the higher level is being coded, a considerable amount of rewriting of lower levels is likely to be needed to correct the fault. The constraints imposed at a low level, often to overcome possible problems that might be encountered at a later stage, are reflected right through the program, and make the higher levels much more complicated than is actually necessary.

The 'top-down' approach, on the other hand, requires that the programmer deals with the overall specification first, before proceeding to the details. Figure 2.2 shows the essential difference between this and the 'bottom-up' approach.

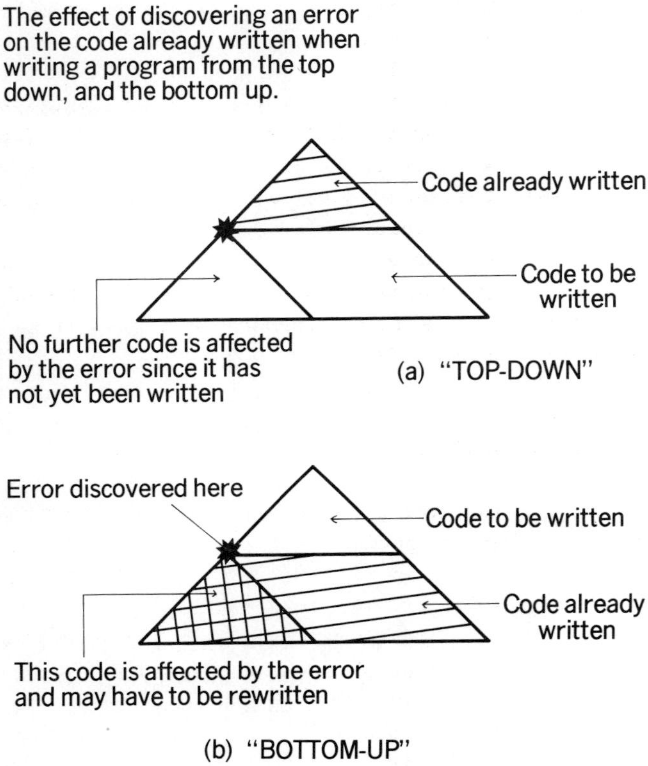

Figure 2.2 The difference between developing a program from the top down, and the bottom up

This allows an error in the design of the program to be corrected before too much work has been spent on trying to implement it. In this way, as little code as possible needs to be rewritten, considerably easing the programming task. Many errors, which are only discovered after coding is completed and the program is being tested, are caused by the programmer not having a complete understanding of the problem he is trying to solve. It is by then too late to make drastic changes to the program without expending a lot of effort on rewriting it. If coding starts only when the problem is properly understood, a considerable amount of anguish will be saved at a later stage.

It is very easy to say how programs should be written, but it is often very difficult to write them in the best possible way. If the user is not completely familiar with the facilities provided, either in the language that he is using, or the computer system on which it is to run, it is essential that he try out different possible solutions. This is best done by writing special trial programs, rather than using the program that is being written. These trial programs should be written in a well structured way so that it is clear what is being tested. In this way, the user can be sure that he is testing what he thinks he is, and is unlikely to find unfortunate side-effects caused by the interaction with other parts of the program. Only when the user is completely sure of what the module is intended to do, and how he is going to make it do it, is it time to start writing the code.

2.3 STRUCTURED PROGRAMMING

The ideas behind 'structured programming' have been discussed widely by academic programming specialists for about ten years, and have been used in commercial programming in an attempt to establish recognised standards.

Programmers are a very individual breed, and everyone of us has his own way of solving common problems. In the early days of computing it was indeed usual for programmers to go out of their way to write confusing and unfathomable code to gain some, often mythical, speed or storage advantage. 'Individual' programming was fine so long as the programmer was still around to sort out any problems that arose once the program was in regular use. But what if he left the company or was working on another project? Someone else would have to work his way through each step of the code and try to find a solution. This search for the needle in a haystack frequently meant that it was cheaper to rebuild the program from scratch.

With the coming of microcomputer software, the problems of maintainance are far greater since the program is likely to be distributed to many users, widely spread geographically, with few specialist programmers immediately available in the locality. If the program is distributed in read-only memory the problems are even greater. For, since issuing corrective patches is impossible, new memories must be manufactured and released through the dealer network, with all the extra costs that ensue. It is, therefore, essential that if programs are to be maintained, the originator should have reasonable confidence in their ability to work in a normal user environment from the start. If problems occur later, no matter from what cause, their effects should be limited to as small an area as possible so that the true cause can be isolated, and dealt with quickly.

There is always the temptation, when a program fails, and you are under pressure to get your microcomputer working, to deal with the symptoms rather than the cause of the problem. This is highly dangerous, since you are sowing the seeds of another failure, which will be much more difficult to rectify since the patches will now get in the way.

As with many other tasks, programming is best approached in a systematic way. With the simple problems that will be discussed in the earlier chapters of this book, it is possible to grasp the whole problem and its solution in one step. When writing programs which are intended to solve real problems, it is very rare for them to be this concise. The complete problem must, therefore, be split into a number of subsidiary ones that can then be solved independently. If any of these are themselves too large to be tackled in one attempt, they can themselves be broken down until each section can be handled comfortably. Programming should be seen, therefore, not as a monolithic task that must be performed in one go, but as a series of subsidiary goals that can be tackled one by one, until the complete program is ready.

Structured programming is a way of ensuring that these subsidiary sections are arranged in such a way that they can be worked on truly independently, that is, without reference to other parts of the program. In this way each section can be tested and debugged as it is completed, thus considerably enhancing the chances of obtaining a working program. In addition, if problems do occur, they can be isolated and found very much more easily than in a single, complete program. It is usually only necessary to correct code in the section in which the problem occurred, so that reprogramming can also be minimised.

So a structured program must be made up of a series of sections, each of which should:

(a) perform only one specified task
(b) complete the task satisfactorily before continuing
(c) have only one entry point
(d) have only one exit
(e) be composed of the necessary program statements, or calls to other sub-sections which perform various sub-tasks and which

themselves strictly satisfy these conditions.

(f) be independent and not include jumps into code which is included in other sections, since this would violate the rule on entry points and exits.

If these rules are followed correctly, each section of a program could be coded as separate sections or sub-routines. But this is rather extreme and would make the program as a whole rather difficult to follow. It is therefore usual to define sub-routines for those tasks which are likely to be called in several places, or when the task is so important that its programming is a major step forward towards the completion of the project.

No programmer can be fully familiar with the whole of even a moderately complex program for the total time required to write, test and debug it. Sections should therefore be of a size that can be worked on comfortably. It is often convenient to restrict the length of each sub-routine to at most one page of printer output or a couple of screen displays on a video terminal, since this is a convenient amount of text to study and edit. Indeed, to encourage this, most PASCAL compilers limit the amount of code that can be generated in any one program section, and give a compiler error message if this is exceeded.

2.4 THE STRUCTURE OF A PROGRAM

It has been realised for some time that only three control structures are required to write any program. They are:

(a) the sequence,
(b) the condition, and
(c) the loop.

Apart from the sequence, in which program statements are executed one after the other (see figure 2.3), most programming languages allow the programmer alternative constructions of each.

While only one construction of each type is actually required to write any program, this would be at the expense of clarity. Allowing a limited number of alternatives leads to simpler, and much more elegant programs.

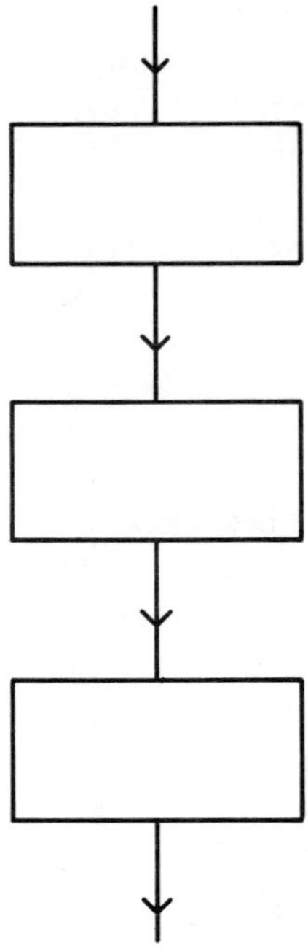

Figure 2.3 The sequence

The condition allows you to write programs which can deal with a number of different situations. Without it, a different program would be needed to handle every minor variation in the specification to which the program was written. This would make all computers far too inflexible for use in all but a very few cases.

Conditions can be further sub-divided into the following classes:

(a) single branched,
(b) double branched, and
(c) multiple branched.

The simplest form of condition is the single-branched variety, which has the general form:

```
IF <condition> THEN
     <do something>
```

In fact, all algorithms can be expressed as a special form of the one branch condition, known as the single-branched instruction, where the 'body' of the condition (that is the part which is executed if the stated condition is met) is a jump to another part of the program. This is, in fact, the only type of condition which is

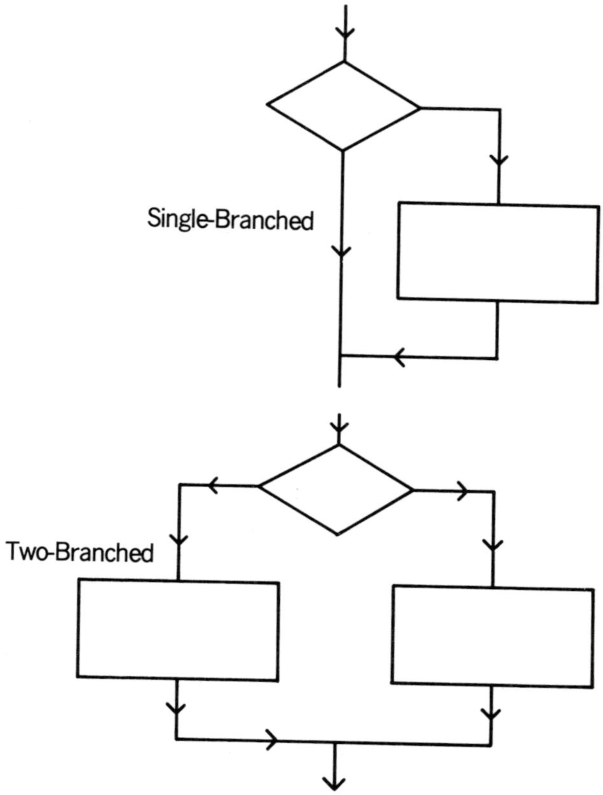

Figure 2.4 The condition

present in most microprocessors' instruction sets. Early programming languages followed this construction, so that only, for instance, with the latest FORTRAN compilers is there a two-branched condition of the form:

```
IF <condition> THEN
     <do something>
ELSE
     <do something else>
```

and very few BASIC interpreters allow this type of statement. Since many algorithms are of the form that one of two alternative routes are to be followed, depending on the result of some test, this is a major deficiency of many of the languages commonly used on microcomputers. In block-structured languages the body of the condition can be made up of a number of statements, making the construction very powerful indeed.

The multi-branched condition is used when there are a number of possible alternatives, depending on the value of some variable. This avoids the necessity of using a number of single- or double-branched conditions, nested one within the other, like, for instance,

```
IF <variable>=<value1> THEN
     <do something>
ELSE
     IF <variable>=<value2> THEN
          <do something else>
     ELSE
        IF <variable>=<value3> THEN
             <do something else again>
```

which can be very confusing to read.

Using a multi-branched condition , this can be written much more compactly, as:

```
CASE <variable> OF
   <value1> : <do something>
   <value2> : <do something else>
   <value3> : <do something else again>
END;
```

This is commonly called the 'CASE' construction because of the keyword used in many programming languages, including PASCAL, to introduce it.

Computers are most useful when they are used to repeat the same calculation a large number of times. This is accomplished using the various forms of the loop construction. The most common ones are:

(a) loop while some condition is met,
(b) repeat until some condition is met, possibly for ever, and
(c) loop a set number of times.

The flow of control is shown in figure 2.5.

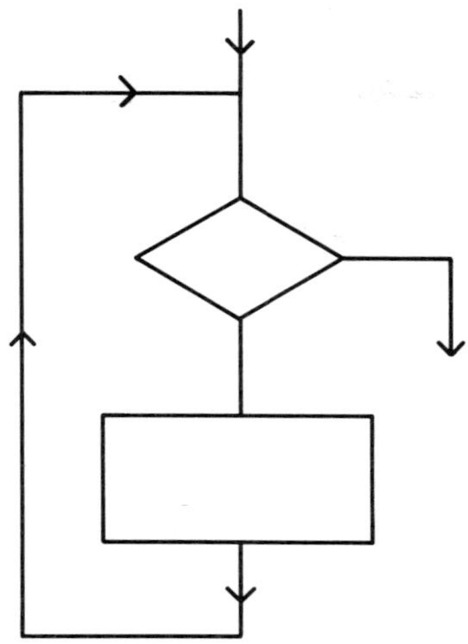

Figure 2.5 The loop

The essential difference between the 'while' loop and the 'repeat' loop is in where the test for completion is made. In the case of the 'while' loop, the test is made before the first execution of the body of the loop. If the condition is not met on entry into the loop, the loop body is not executed at all, whereas in the case of the 'repeat' loop the condition is tested after execution of the body of the loop. This means that for the 'repeat' loop the body of the loop will always be executed at least once, no matter whether the condition is met or not. In most languages, the condition must be met for continued execution of the 'while' loop, giving a construction of the form:

```
WHILE <condition> DO
     <do something>
```

In the case of the 'repeat' loop, on the other hand, the loop is executed until some condition is reached, giving a construction of the form:

```
REPEAT
     <do something>
UNTIL <condition>
```

It is sometimes useful to tell the microcomputer that a certain section of code is to be executed a set number of times. This can be done by setting up a loop with a 'while' or 'repeat' loop, and using a counter to determine how many times the loop is to be executed. A suitable scheme would look something like this:

```
counter := <number of times loop is to be executed>
WHILE counter >= 0 DO
     <do something>
     counter := counter-1
<continue processing>
```

As will be seen, this is a somewhat awkward way of performing what is, in practice, quite a common operation. It is usual, therefore, to provide another type of loop, known as the 'for' loop, for just this eventuality. This allows the programmer to specify the range over which some loop or control variable is to be stepped for each loop, or iteration. The form taken is:

```
FOR <loop variable>:=<lower bound> TO <upper bound> DO
     <do something>
```

In PASCAL, the loop variable is stepped by one each time it is executed.

2.5 DEVELOPING PROGRAMS

A great temptation when writing any program is to think that it will be needed only once, and therefore that no great care is required in its design and programming. This is a great mistake. Any program is potentially a valuable addition to a program library, and may be swapped or sold to other users with a similar problem to solve. So it is essential that the program is carefully constructed from the start, as otherwise it may have to be effectively rewritten before full use can be made of it.

Professional programming managers have shown great interest in structured programming concepts as a way of simplifying the writing of programs, and also in easing the problems associated with changing them once they are in regular use. All large computer installations have large staffs of programmers, much of whose time is taken up maintaining the programs in regular use on their computer system. Not only do errors have to be rectified as soon as they are discovered, but programs have to be rewritten to reflect the changes in their use and to take advantage of any new facilities that become available during their working life.

All programmers implicitly believe that there are no bugs in their programs, and indeed, it can well be argued that a bug does not exist until it has been found, but as every computer manager knows, problems are soon discovered when any new program is put into everyday operation. A microcomputer user has to be his own computer manager, discovering and isolating bugs in programs and hardware, and his own programmer, having to put them right. He does not have a large staff of systems analysts and programmers to do the job for him. Most of the discussion about structured programming has centred around the cost and staff savings that can be made by adopting these techniques. In the microcomputer world it is impossible to save on a staff of only yourself, but it is possible to save a considerable amount of time by adopting similar techniques, without, necessarily, purchasing expensive software products.

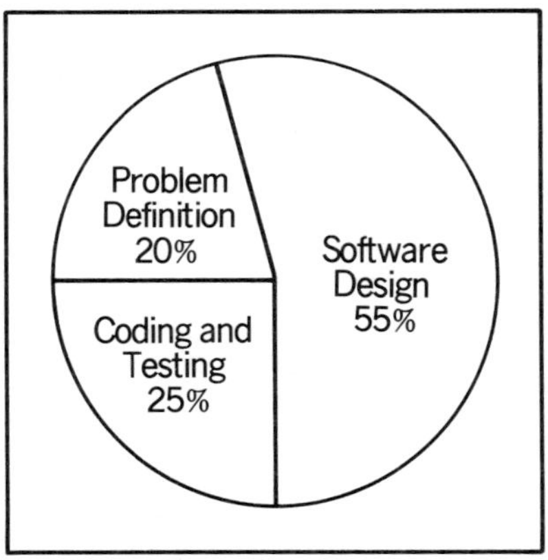

Figure 2.6 The amount of time spent on the various tasks required to write a complete program

As figure 2.6 shows, much of the time taken to develop a program is in the initial design stage. It is then that the method of representing the data, and the general algorithm to be used when writing the program, must be decided upon. All this must be done before any code can be written. As a general rule, any program goes through a number of clearly defined stages before becoming a useful addition to the library of working programs. These stages can be defined as follows:

(a) System specification - defining what the program is intended to do.
(b) Program design - the most significant part, planning how the program can be written to meet the objectives defined in (a).
(c) Detailed coding - actually writing the program code.
(d) Testing and debugging - the most important part, making sure that the program does precisely what it is intended to do.
(e) The program must then be integrated with the other programs in use to form part of the overall system.
(f) Documentation - telling yourself and others who might want to use your program how to do so. The documentation should also contain information on how to maintain the program, should this be necessary.

As is shown in figure 2.7, the main effort is concentrated on the implementation stages. This is when the detailed design is

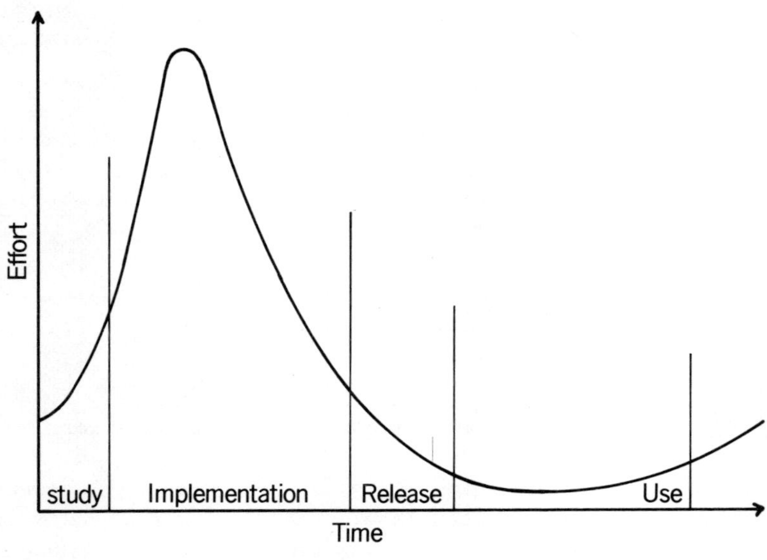

Figure 2.7 The effort required at the various stages of development

completed, and the actual coding and initial testing is performed. After the initial testing phase is complete, the effort needed to complete the task drops enormously as the final integration problems are sorted out. Once the program is in general use, the effort required to maintain it does not fall off entirely as some problems are still likely to occur. However, if the design work was carried out carefully these should be minimal. As the program ages, more problems are likely to occur as different parts of the system are upgraded. Again, if the design of the program was good these will be accommodated with the minimum maintainance effort. Eventually there will come a point where, either the changes required are too great, or the program has been butchered so much, or the program must be moved to a very different operating environment, that the effort required to maintain the program is so great that it is far easier to rewrite it from scratch. It must be the object of all microcomputer programmers to design and write programs which will run with the minimum maintainance effort for, at least, the expected life of their microcomputer. This can be done very easily, so long as adequate time and effort is expended at the initial design stage.

2.6 THE ELEMENTS OF 'TOP-DOWN' DESIGN

The basic principles of top-down design can be given as a series of statements, as follows:

(a) Design the program in levels
The program is designed in a series of levels, each of which is completed before work starts on the next. Each module can be completed, and tested, by including just the stubs of those modules which are yet to be written at the lower levels. In this way most of the bugs can be removed as the program is written, because it should always be possible to compile it and run at least some tests. Figure 2.8 shows how a program might be developed in a series of levels.

(b) Initial language independence
The first description of the program is usually written in such a way as to relate to the problem in mind, and cannot be directly converted into code. It may, indeed, be written totally in English. This allows the programmer to choose the most appropriate language in which to write the complete program, and indeed in some cases, as will be seen in the next chapter, each level.

(c) Postponement of details to the lower levels
The broad issues should be settled at the higher levels, leaving

the detailed implementation decisions to lower ones. This allows the programmer to concentrate on the most important

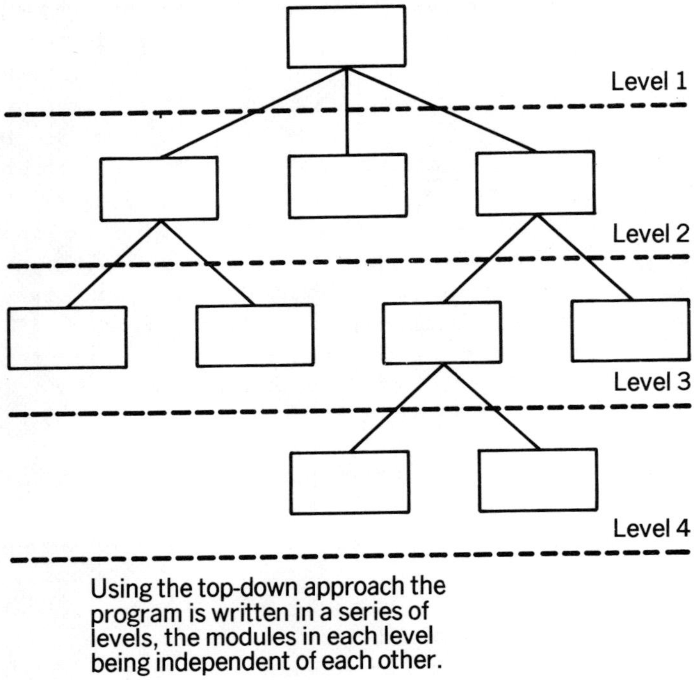

Figure 2.8 Designing a program in levels

points at the beginning, the details of implementation being left until he needs to write the detailed code.

(d) Defining the interface with the lower levels
At each level it is necessary to define the interface with the levels below. When it comes to writing a module, its complete function is therefore known. This ensures that each module can be written independently, and that the interfaces will not require changes at later stages.

(e) Verification of each level, as it is written
Each level can be verified before going on to the next. This is most important because errors can then be detected, and corrected, before they can do any real harm, saving many hours

of debugging effort.

In this way the program can be developed, and tested, with the minimum of trouble. Figure 2.9 shows the difference in the way in

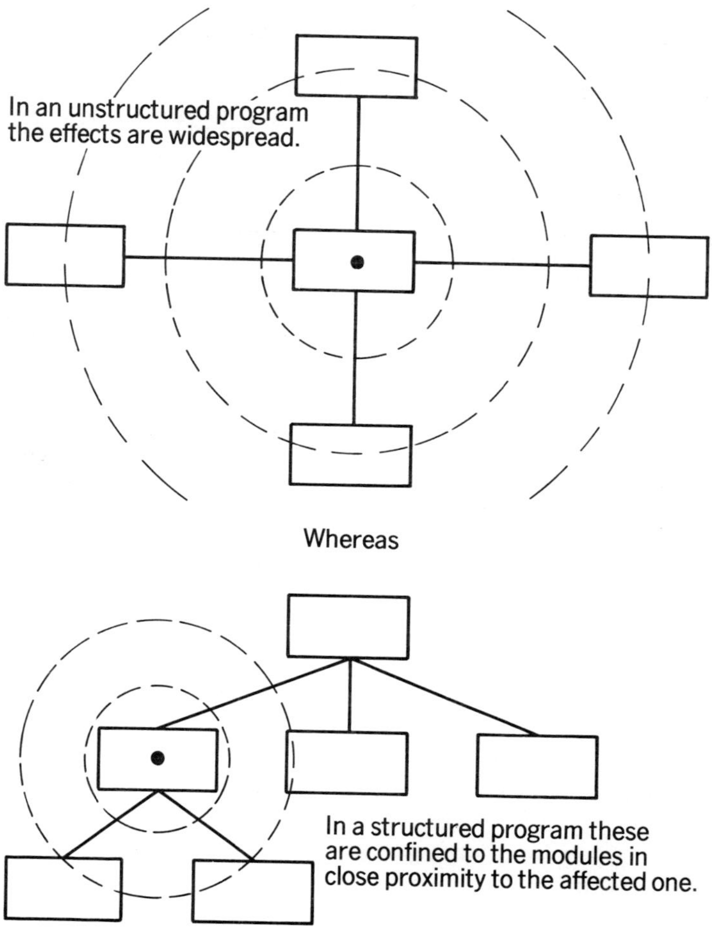

Figure 2.9 The effects of an error in a structured and an unstructured program

which a program error permeates round a structured and an unstructured program. In an unstructured program the effects of a single error can be found in all sorts of places, making any attempt at finding its cause very difficult. With a structured program, however, the effects are confined to those modules in close proximity to the one containing the error. This gives the programmer a lot of useful information about the source of the error, that he can use to track down and correct the module in question.

As was shown in figure 2.1, a program is simply a representation of a real-life problem, in terms that are amenable to computational solution. During the useful life of the program, it is likely that the problem will change. It might be that, for instance, an accounts program must now handle another type of tax that the government has just introduced. If the program were not written in a modular fashion, it would have to be totally rewritten, whereas if it were, only those modules affected would require attention. A considerable amount of work would probably be saved because much of the workings of the program would be totally unaffected. It is not always possible to predict what changes may be necessary during the life of a program, but a proper modular structure will go a long way towards ensuring that it can be adequately maintained until its usefulness is finished.

2.7 PROBLEMS

2.1 It is intended to write a program to keep a list of all the equipment in a laboratory. Define a method for doing this, and outline the modules that would be needed.

2.2 What are the main control structures required to write any program?

2.3 What is the essential difference between a 'while' loop and a 'repeat' loop?

2.4 Where is the most time and effort expended when designing and writing a program?

2.5 Consider what needs to be done when a program requires amendment to meet some new operating criteria. Where do you think that most effort will be required?

CHAPTER 3
The Basics of PASCAL

3.1 THE ELEMENTS OF A PASCAL PROGRAM

It is now time to look at how programs are written in PASCAL, so that they can be entered into the microcomputer's backing store, and translated into machine code ready for execution. Each program consists of keywords and special symbols, both of which are defined as part of the PASCAL language, and are therefore valid in all programs written in PASCAL, and identifiers, which must be defined by the programmer at the start of each program, or section of a program, and which may only be used within that program, or section. To identify keywords within program examples, capital letters will be used for them, and small letters will be used for identifiers, both when they are defined, and when they are subsequently used.

A PASCAL program consists of a program heading, which tells the host computer's operating system the things it needs to know about it, and the main text, or body. The heading starts with the keyword PROGRAM and the name of the program. The input and output units to be used are also listed, in brackets, following the program name, since this is information which is needed by many operating systems. In most simple programs the only units to be used are those required for standard input and output, which on a typical microcomputer would be the main console keyboard and the video display. These have been predefined by the system designer as 'input' and 'output' respectively. Since they are predefined identifiers, and not keywords defined as part of the PASCAL language, they are printed in small letters. If other units were required to be used instead of the keyboard and display, their identifiers would need to be specified in the heading, instead of 'input' and 'output'.

The way in which a program is laid out, when listed, is very important to the human reader. However, it is of absolutely no meaning to the microcomputer, or to the compiler which reads the program as a long sequence of characters in the order that they were entered into memory. Good layout is therefore very important, since it can make the underlying structure of the program very much clearer to another person reading your program, and to you youself when you come back to a program you wrote several months ago and wish to find out what, exactly, it was supposed to do. In PASCAL, spaces and new lines are not significant, except when they are used to separate individual words, or symbols, within the program. This is to allow the programmer to lay out his programs in the most appropriate way to show the overall structure, and to make it as clear and as readable as possible. It does mean however that a single statement can spread over a number of lines, or that several statements may be most appropriately placed on a single line, depending on the layout of the program. A statement separator must therefore be used when it is not obvious where one statement ends and another begins. A semi-colon (;) is used for this purpose. This therefore is the heading for our first program, which shall be called 'first':

```
PROGRAM first(input,output);
```

This first program (program 3.1) will print this message on the principal output device (probably the display screen):

```
this is a very simple PASCAL program
```

In this case, only one program statement is required to write out the message, and then start a new line.

It is not necessary, in this example, to declare any further identifiers, so the text of the program follows immediately after the PROGRAM heading. The text of the program is enclosed between the keywords 'BEGIN' and 'END', to indicate that this is the part that is actually executed. After the 'END' a full stop (.) is used rather than a semi-colon to indicate that this is really the end of the program. The full program now, therefore, will look something like this:

```
PROGRAM printit(input,output);

BEGIN
     <do something>
END.
```

All that is needed now is the code to write out the message. In

PASCAL there are two write statements:

```
write(<list of things to be written>)
```

and

```
writeln(<list of things to be written>)
```

(both 'write' and 'writeln' are in small letters because they are not keywords in PASCAL). The difference between the two is that 'write' simply writes out the items specified in the output list without generating a new line, whereas 'writeln' writes out all the items in the list, and then writes a new line character. In this case it is necessary to use 'writeln' because some output devices, notably printers, do not actually display what is sent to them until a new line character is received.

The message to be written is:

```
this is a very simple PASCAL program
```

Since this is to be printed exactly as it stands it must be enclosed in single quotes ('). The complete program is given in program 3.1.

```
PROGRAM first (input,output);

BEGIN
   writeln('THIS IS A VERY SIMPLE PASCAL PROGRAM')
END.
```

Program 3.1 The first program

If this program is run on your microcomputer system, the text of the program will probably appear in the midst of a whole range of system messages, designed to tell you what the microcomputer is doing in order to run the program. It may well be quite difficult to find, and therefore you might be unsure whether the program has, in fact, executed correctly or not. Since most of the system messages are unnecessary if the program executes successfully, it would be much more sensible to clear the screen at the start of the program, then only those messages actually generated by the program would appear on the screen.

PASCAL provides another predefined procedure, similar to 'write' and 'writeln', to do just this. It may be called in the following way:

```
page(output)
```

where the file identifier (in this case, output) appears in brackets. This is necessary in order that the same procedure may be used with any output file. 'Page' is also, for instance, used to throw a new page on a printer. In this case the name of the printing device would be used rather than output. Program 3.2 shows how 'page' can be used to clear the video screen, so that only the message appears. Many of the example programs will do this, so that the messages displayed are not confused with anything else that had been displayed previously.

```
PROGRAM first (input,output);

BEGIN
   page(output);
   writeln;
   writeln;
   writeln('THIS IS A VERY SIMPLE PASCAL PROGRAM')
END.
```

Program 3.2 The first program, modified to clear the screen before displaying the message

3.2 SIMPLE CALCULATIONS

There are very few applications that can be satisfied as easily as this. Programs are usually written to manipulate data, either in a way that is too complex to be done directly, or when such large quantities are involved that it would be very time-consuming to handle it in any other way. If the value of the data is known at the time that the program is written, it can be included as a constant. This allows the programmer to define non-varying data as part of the program, rather than having to ask the user for it, or obtaining it from some other source.

With constants, it is necessary to associate the identifier name, by which it is to be known throughout the program, with its intended value. In PASCAL, constants are declared at the start of the program, between the heading and the start of the main program. To identify them as constant declarations, they are used with the keyword CONST. The skeleton of a program that is to use constants declared at compilation would therefore be:

```
PROGRAM constants(input,output);

CONST
   <constant declarations>;

BEGIN
   <statements to be executed>
END.
```

If, for instance, the two numbers 3 and 4 are to be added together, they could be declared as:

```
CONST
    number1=3;
    number2=4;
```

Henceforth these numbers can be referred to by name in the program. While, in this case, the advantage may be marginal, this facility allows the programmer to make his programs very adaptable to differing environments, since if various constant limits, such as, for instance, the number of lines on a page of output, or the number of characters to be printed on each line, are declared as constants at the top of the program, it is a very simple task to change them, and then recompile the program, rather than to find each instance of the limits being checked within the program text, and altering each of those.

In PASCAL, names are allocated by the programmer, and must be formed from a letter, followed by any number of letters, or digits. This allows meaningful names to be given. It should however be noted that most compilers currently in use recognise only the first few characters of each name, often eight, to save memory space at the compilation stage, and to allow more rapid compilation. This means that care must be taken to ensure that these letters are different for each name. There is no reason, however, why the full name should not be used. Program 3.3 shows how the computer can be used to add two numbers together.

```
PROGRAM add1(input,output);

CONST
   numb1 = 3;
   numb2 = 4;

BEGIN
   writeln(numb1,' + ',numb2,' = ',numb1+numb2)
END.
```

Program 3.3 A program to add two numbers together

3.3 WRITING PROGRAMS TO INTERACT WITH THE MICROCOMPUTER USER

It is possible to perform quite complex calculations in this way, but every time a new calculation is attempted, the program must be rewritten, and compiled again. This would be very inconvenient in practice, since in most cases it is only worthwhile writing a program if the calculation is to be performed a number of times, each time with different data. It is better therefore if the program can be written so that the data can be entered from the microcomputer keyboard when the program requests it. In this way the program can be used many times without recompilation.

To do this, it is necessary to enter the data into the microcomputer's memory, where it can be manipulated by the program as required. The programmer must tell the compiler what memory is required, so that it can be allocated automatically. Not only must the number of variables and their names be given at the start of the program, but also the sort of data that is to be stored. This is necessary as, before storage can be allocated, certain things must be known about the information it is to contain. This includes:

(a) how much space is required to store the information (i.e. how many bytes of information (see page 40) are required).
(b) what type of data is to be stored, so that the storage allocated can be arranged in the most appropriate way.
(c) a name, which will be used in the rest of the program to identify that storage area when information is to be stored there or retrieved from it later in the program.

The programmer gives this information to the compiler in the variable declarations at the start of his program. PASCAL enforces very rigid rules as to the order of declarations at the start of the program. All constant declarations must be grouped together immediately after the PROGRAM heading, and then all the variable declarations must follow, introduced by the keyword 'VAR'. Each declaration is separated from the next by a semi-colon.

The program will now look like this:

```
PROGRAM constantsandvariables(input,output);

CONST
   <constant declarations>;

VAR
   <variable declarations>;

BEGIN
   <statements to be executed>
END.
```

Variable declarations are laid out somewhat differently from constant declarations, because they convey different information to the compiler. The identifier name is given first, followed by a colon (:), and then the data type of the information to be stored. So, for instance, the space required to store a single integer value would be reserved by the following delaration:

```
VAR
   numb1 : integer;
```

Later in the program this space would be referred to by its name, numb1.

If a number of memory spaces in which integers are to be stored must be declared at the start of the program, they can be reserved in one statement by listing all the identifier names, separated by commas, before the colon. That is, for instance, like this:

```
VAR
   numb1, numb2 : integer;
```

Now the program to add two numbers together can be revised, so that the numbers are typed in from the keyboard after each of their values is requested by a message displayed on a terminal, and the value is then displayed. It is most important that a program should tell whoever is running it, not only when it requires the user to input some data from the terminal, but also what data is required, and in what form the microcomputer will accept it. This is best done by arranging for the program to display some text, as a prompt, on the screen, immediately before the program requires that it is to be read in. Once all the data that is required to perform the programmed task has been read in, the result can be calculated, and displayed for the user to read. Program 3.4 shows how this can be done.

```
PROGRAM add2(input,output);

VAR
   numb1,numb2 : integer;

BEGIN
   page(output);
   writeln('A PROGRAM TO ADD TWO NUMBERS TOGETHER');
   writeln;
   writeln;
   write('ENTER THE FIRST NUMBER -->');
   readln(numb1);
   writeln;
   write('ENTER THE SECOND NUMBER -->');
   readln(numb2);
   writeln;
   writeln;
   writeln(numb1,' + ',numb2,' = ',numb1+numb2)
END.
```

Program 3.4 A program to read two numbers from the keyboard, add them together, and display the result

Program 3.4 shows the basic skeleton of many more. First, some data is read into the microcomputer's memory, some processing is then performed using it, and finally, the results must be displayed in a form that is acceptable to the user. Most programs follow this basic form, and it is important to remember that the only information that the average user is interested in is the final result. It is to obtain this that he has run your program, and if insufficient, or worse still, wrong information is supplied back to him, he will not be enthusiastic about using it again.

3.4 PROBLEMS

3.1 Which of the following are valid PASCAL identifiers?

a	1list
length	first-side
?height	area1
2nd-side	compare2strings
compare two strings	list.two
a3	area4

State the reasons why you consider them to be valid.

3.2 Write a PASCAL program to clear the screen, and write the message:

this is my first PASCAL program

on the principal output device of your microcomputer.

3.3 Write a PASCAL program to subtract the number 10 from the number 47.

3.4 Write a PASCAL program which reads two integers from the keyboard, multiplies them together, and displays the result on the microcomputer's main output device. (The multiplication operator is represented by *.)

CHAPTER 4
Using Data Types

4.1 STORING DATA WITHIN THE COMPUTER

Before a program can process any information, it must first be entered into the microcomputer and stored in the main memory. It is necessary, therefore, for the programmer to specify exactly how this information is to be stored, as well as what processing is intended to be performed in it. As has already been shown in Chapter 3, in PASCAL, the program is written in two parts, a series of declarations immediately following the program heading that allocate storage for the various items of data that are to be stored, followed by the instructions that make up the program itself.

The microcomputer's memory is made up of a series of individual cells, called bits, each of which can contain one item of information. The contents of each cell can, in fact, only be a one or a zero. One cell can therefore be used to store data which has only two values (for instance true and false). It is, however possible to group these cells together and store other information in a coded form. All programs and data stored within the computer are, in fact, stored in this way.

The differences between the various types of information stored within the memory are in the number of bits used, and in what, exactly, they represent. Most microcomputer memories are arranged in such a way that the bits are grouped together in eights. This is particularly convenient because there are two hundred and fifty-six possible combinations of the contents of these eight bits. This is more than sufficient to provide one code for each of the different printing characters, and the control functions associated with peripherals and communications, notably the types of printer which can be connected to computers. Each group of eight bits is given a special name, a byte.

When data is transferred to and from the microprocessor, it is, in fact, moved in blocks of eight, i.e. one byte at a time. For these codes to have any real value, all computers, and the printers, terminals and other devices connected to them, must use the same codes to represent each character or control function otherwise it would be impossible to read, manipulate and print text in any reliable, systematic way. This was realised in the early days of computing, and a number of different 'standard codes' have been developed over the years to include all the useful characters and control messages. The final result, in the late 1960s, was the American Standard Codes for Information Interchange, ASCII for short, and it is these codes that are used to represent characters within almost all of the current range of microcomputer systems. (A full list of ASCII codes is given in Appendix A.)

With numbers, a limit of two hundred and fifty-six different codes would be very restricting. It is therefore usual to use two, or more, bytes to allow a sufficient range of different possibilities to be represented. If two bytes are used, for instance, there are 2^{16}, or 65535 possible different numbers that can be represented, sufficient, for instance, to cover all the integers in the range -32827 to +32828. This is more than sufficient for most purposes.

4.2 INTEGER VARIABLES

Integer variables were met briefly in the last chapter. Many quantities that need to be stored and manipulated within the computer are basically counts of the number of a particular item. This type of data can be adequately represented as an integer variable.

Not only must variables be stored, but it must be possible to perform calculations on them so that useful results can be obtained. The operations required to obtain these results are programmed in assignment statements, which have the general form:

<variable> := <arithmetic expression>

where the arithmetic expression yields a result of the same type as the variable that it is to be assigned to. Thus if the variable is declared within the program to be an integer, the result of the arithmetic expression must also be an integer.

In PASCAL it is possible to perform the following arithmetic operations on integers.

```
    +      addition,
    -      subtraction,
    *      multiplication,
    DIV    division
and MOD    take the modulus.
```

Typical assignment statements would therefore look like this:

```
feet := 12 * inches;
balance := credits - debits;
remainder := items MOD 12;
```

Program 4.1 adds two integers together, and finds their difference. The actual work is done by the two assignment statements, in which the values to be stored in 'sum' and 'diff' are calculated, before being printed out.

```
PROGRAM sumanddiff(input,output);

VAR
   num1,num2 : integer;
   sum,diff : integer;

BEGIN
   page(output);
   writeln;
   writeln;
   writeln('A PROGRAM TO DISPLAY THE SUM AND');
   writeln('DIFFERENCE OF TWO INTEGERS');
   writeln;
   writeln;
   write('ENTER THE FIRST NUMBER -->');
   readln(num1);
   writeln;
   write('ENTER THE SECOND NUMBER -->');
   readln(num2);
   writeln;
   writeln;
   sum := num1 + num2;
   writeln('THE SUM OF ',num1,' AND ',num2,' IS ',sum);
```

```
    diff := num1 - num2;
    writeln('AND THE DIFFERENCE IS ',diff)
  END.
```

Program 4.1 A program to read two integers from the keyboard and display their sum and difference

Where two or more operators are required within an expression,. an order of evaluation is required. The rules of evaluation follow those of normal arithmetic, i.e. that the operators

    *   DIV and MOD

have a higher precedence than

    + and -

Otherwise operators of the same precedence are normally executed from left to right. Thus, for example,

```
result := i - j * k;
```

would be evaluated as follows, if i = 12, j = 5 and k = 2:

    5 * 2 = 10
    12 + 10 = 22

and so the value stored in result, after the execution of this assignment statement, is 22.

If these rules are inadequate, round brackets may be used by the programmer to define the order of evaluation explicitly. A slightly modified form of the last example would be:

```
result := ( i - j ) * k;
```

this would be evaluated as follows:

    12 - 5 = 7
     7 * 2 = 14

so the value stored in result, following this assignment statement, would be 14.

Program 4.2 shows how DIV and MOD can be used to obtain the result of an integer division, together with the remainder.

```
PROGRAM divandrem(input,output);

VAR
   num1,num2 : integer;
   result,remainder : integer;

BEGIN
   page(output);
   writeln;
   writeln;
   writeln('A PROGRAM TO DISPLAY THE RESULT OF');
   write('OF THE DIVISION OF TWO INTEGERS,');
      writeln(' AND THE REMAINDER.');
   writeln;
   writeln;
   write('ENTER THE FIRST NUMBER -->');
   readln(num1);
   writeln;
   write('ENTER THE SECOND NUMBER -->');
   readln(num2);
   writeln;
   writeln;
   result := num1 DIV num2;
   writeln('DIVIDING  ',num1,' BY ',num2,' GIVES ',result);
   remainder := num1 MOD num2;
   writeln('AND THE REMAINDER  IS ',remainder)
END.
```

Program 4.2 A program to read two integers from the keyboard, and display the result of the first divided by the second, together with the remainder

In addition, a number of more complex calculations are required so often that it is worth including the facilities for performing them within the programming language itself. This is done by the provision of standard functions, which are used in place of variable names within an arithmetic expression. There are a number of standard functions which yield integer results if the argument, i, is an integer expression.

```
abs(i)          yields the absolute value of i
                i.e. abs(i) becomes i if i is  positive and
                abs(i) becomes -i if i is negative.
sqr(i)          yields the square of i.
```

and so, for instance, the following can be written:

```
isquared := sqr( i );
```

or

```
positivevalue := abs( i ) + 1;
```

4.3 THE USE OF SCALARS

It is often the case that the data required to solve a particular problem is not conveniently represented by one of the conventional data types. PASCAL provides a very useful facility whereby the values that can be taken by a variable can be defined by the programmer. This gives the flexibility that is needed, either to define the specific values that can be taken, or to specify a whole range of allowable values. If this is done, any attempt to assign a value outside this range to the variable will result in an immediate execution error, thus identifying the problem immediately. For example,

```
VAR
   side : (left,right);
   colour : (blue,red,yellow);
   datatype : (integervalue,realvalue,charvalue);
```

the allowable values of a particular variable may be specified within that declaration, e.g.

```
VAR
   bit1 : 0..1;
   firstbyte : 0..255;
```

declares two variables, bit1, which may contain the values 0 and 1 only, and the variable firstbyte, which can contain any value between 0 and 255.

In program 4.3, scalars are used to declare suitable variables in which to store the numbers of both feet and inches, which must fall within specific ranges. If there were an error in the logic of the program which resulted in a value outside the specified range, an error would be signalled immediately, considerably assisting the diagnosis and rectification of the problem.

```
PROGRAM convert(input,output);

VAR
   yards : integer;
   feet  : 0..3;
   inches: 0..12;
   noinches : integer;

BEGIN
   page(output);
   writeln;
   writeln;
   writeln('A PROGRAM TO CONVERT YARDS, FEET,');
   writeln('AND INCHES, INTO INCHES.');
   writeln;
   writeln;
   write('HOW MANY YARDS? -->');
   readln(yards);
   write('HOW MANY FEET? -->');
   readln(feet);
   write('HOW MANY INCHES? -->');
   readln(inches);
   writeln;
   writeln;
   noinches := (yards*3+feet)*12+inches;
   writeln(noinchesa,' INCHES IS EQUIVALENT TO');
   writeln(yards,'YARDS,',feet,'FEET, AND,',inches,'INCHES.')
END.
```

Program 4.3 A program to convert a length given in yards, feet and inches, into inches

4.4 THE DECLARATION OF DATA TYPES

If several variables are to have the same type declarations, it is often more convenient to separate the definition of data type from the variable declaration itself. PASCAL allows the programmer to do this in a very convenient way, using TYPE declarations. E.g.

```
TYPE
   bit = 0..1;
   byte = 0..255;

VAR
   bit1 : bit;
   firstbyte : byte;
```

has the same effect as the declarations discussed in section 4.3.

4.5 THE ORDER OF DECLARATIONS

The order in which constants, data types, and variables are declared is important, in that each can only be used after they have been declared. In PASCAL, this is enforced by requiring that all constants are declared together, followed by all the data types that are to be used within the program, and finally the variables are declared, also together. This allows the programmer to use any constant within a data type definition, and any data type or constant, when defining a variable. A typical program would therefore have a series of declarations laid out in this way:

```
PROGRAM declarations (input,output);

CONST
   <constant declarations>;

TYPE
   <type declarations>;

VAR
   <variable declarations>;

BEGIN
   <program statements>
END.
```

4.6 REAL VARIABLES

In addition to integers and scalars, PASCAL allows the programmer to represent data in the form of real constants and variables.

Real constants are written as a series of digits which include a decimal point. The compiler recognises the difference between integer and real numeric constants by whether or not they include a decimal point. So, for instance, a constant written as 5.0 would be recognised by the compiler as representing a real constant, and 5 on its own would be recognised as an integer.

The arithmetic operations that can be performed on real numbers are as follows:

+	addition
-	subtraction
*	multiplication
/	division

Program 4.4 shows how real numbers can be used. It is often necessary to calculate the value added tax which is payable on a purchase. This program asks the user to supply the price of the item. It then calculates both the tax payable, and the total bill. All three values are then displayed for the user to read. Since the rate of value added tax remains the same for considerable periods, it is defined as a constant. When the tax rate does change, however, it is necessary to modify the program very rapidly, otherwise it will quickly become obsolete. This can be done very easily by changing the constant declaration at the start of the program, and recompiling it.

```
PROGRAM vat(input,output);

CONST
   vatrate = 15.0;

VAR
   price : real;
   tax   : real;

BEGIN
   page(output);
```

```
   writeln;
   writeln('VAT CALCULATION PROGRAM');
   writeln('=== =========== =======');
   writeln;
   writeln;
   write('ENTER THE PRICE -->');
   readln(price);
   page(output);
   writeln;
   writeln('THE PRICE IS   ',price);
   tax := price*(vatrate/100.0);
   price := price+tax;
   writeln('VAT IS          ',tax);
   writeln('PRICE INC. VAT ',price)
END.
```

Program 4.4 A program to calculate the price of an item including value added tax, given its pre-tax price

As well as the operators, there are a number of standard functions available specifically to manipulate real values. These are:

abs(x)	yields the absolute value of x, i.e. abs(x) becomes x if x is positive and abs(x) becomes -x if x is negative.
sqr(x)	yields the square of x.
sqrt(x)	yields the square root of x.
sin(x), cos(x), arctan(x)	trigonometric functions.
ln(x)	yields the natural logarithm of x.
exp(x)	yields e raised to the xth power.

All of these standard functions yield a result of type integer, so long as the argument is of that type.

```
PROGRAM circle(input,output);

CONST
   pi = 3.1416;

VAR
   radius : real;
   area,circumference : real;

BEGIN
   page(output);
   writeln;
   writeln('A PROGRAM TO CALCULATE THE AREA AND');
   writeln('CIRCUMFERENCE OF A CIRCLE');
   writeln;
   writeln;
   write('WHAT IS THE RADIUS OF THE CIRCLE? -->');
   readln(radius);
   area := pi*sqr(radius);
   circumference := 2.0*radius*pi;
   writeln;
   writeln;
   writeln;
   writeln('THE AREA OF A CIRCLE OF RADIUS ',radius);
   writeln('IS',area,'AND ITS CIRCUMFERENCE IS',circumference)
END.
```

Program 4.5 A program to calculate the area and circumference of a circle, given its radius

Programs 4.5 and 4.6 are two simple examples of programs written to perform useful calculations using real numbers. Program 4.5 calculates the circumference and the area of a circle, given its radius. Pi is declared as a real constant, because its value will not change throughout the program. This ensures that, should any attempt be made to change the value of pi elsewhere in the program, a compilation error will result, warning the user that something is seriously wrong before incorrect results can be generated.

```
PROGRAM wlengthtofreq(input,output);

CONST
   c = 300000000.0; (* FREQUENCY OF LIGHT *)

VAR
   wavelength,frequency : real;

BEGIN
   page(output);
   writeln;
   writeln;
   writeln('A PROGRAM TO GIVE THE FREQUENCY OF ELECTRO-MAGNETIC');
   writeln('RADIATION, GIVEN ITS WAVELENGTH');
   writeln;
   writeln;
   write('ENTER THE WAVELENGTH IN METRES -->');
   readln(wavelength);
   writeln;
   writeln;
   writeln;
   frequency := c/wavelength;
   write('THE FREQUENCY OF RADIATION, WITH A WAVELENGTH OF '
        ,wavelength,' METRES');
   writeln('IS ',frequency,' HERTZ')
END.
```

Program 4.6 A program to convert the wavelength of electromagnetic radiation into frequency units

Program 4.6 converts the wavelength of electromagnetic radiation into its respective frequency using the formula:

$$v = \frac{c}{l}$$

where

	v	is the frequency
	l	is the wavelength
and	c	is the speed of light.

Again c is a constant which is declared at the start of the program.

4.7 CONVERSION BETWEEN DATA TYPES

It is possible, in PASCAL, to assign an integer value to a real variable. The necessary internal conversions, due to the different representations of real and integer data within the microcomputer's memory, are handled automatically by the compiler. It is, however, not possible for the compiler to handle the conversion to the assignment of real data to an integer variable in the same way, because of the need to either round or truncate. PASCAL therefore provides two standard functions that do just this, so that the programmer can choose which he wishes to use in any particular situation:

trunc(x)	yields the largest integer whose absolute value is less than the absolute value of x.
round(x)	yields the integer whose value is closest to x.

The standard routines can be used, for instance, for the conversion of litres into gallons, quarts and pints. For most purposes it is only relevant to quote the nearest whole number of pints to the absolute quantity being converted. Program 4.7 does this perfectly adequately. The number of litres is read as a real number, to allow for the entry of half-litres, etc. The litres are then converted into pints by multiplying them by the relevant conversion factor, and rounding to the nearest whole number of pints (if the next highest number of pints is required, for instance, if a solvent can only be bought in whole pints, then trunc would have to be used, and one would then always have to be added to the result). After the conversion has been done, all that is then required is to calculate the number of gallons and the number of pints left over using the div and mod operators discussed in the last chapter, and to print out the conversion.

```
PROGRAM volumeconvert(input,output);

CONST
   litretopint = 1.76;

VAR
   nogallons,nopints : integer;
   nolitres : real;
```

```
BEGIN
   page(output);
   writeln;
   writeln;
   writeln('A PROGRAM TO CONVERT LITRES INTO');
   writeln('= ======= == ======= ====== ====');
   writeln;
   writeln('         GALLONS AND PINTS.');
   writeln('         ======= === ======');
   writeln;
   writeln;
   write('ENTER THE NUMBER OF LITRES -->');
   readln(nolitres);
   nopints := round(nolitres*litretopint);
   nogallons := nopints DIV 8;
   nopints := nopints MOD 8;
   writeln;
   writeln;
   writeln('IS ',nogallons,' GALLONS AND ',nopints,' PINTS.')
END.
```

Program 4.7 A volume conversion program

4.8 MANIPULATION OF CHARACTERS

It is possible to read and store characters directly in PASCAL, using the data type CHAR. For example,

```
VAR
   ch : char;
```

declares a variable, ch, which will contain one character, usually in the form of its ASCII eight-bit code. Program 4.8 shows how a character can be read from the keyboard and displayed on the video screen.

It is, in addition, possible to include characters as constants within the program. This is done by enclosing the desired character within string quotes ('). For instance, if it was desired to assign

```
PROGRAM displaychar(input,output);

VAR
   ch : char;

BEGIN
   page(output);
   writeln;
   write('TYPE IN ANY CHARACTER -->');
   read(ch);
   writeln;
   writeln;
   writeln('THE CHARACTER YOU TYPED WAS ',ch)
END.
```

Program 4.8 A program to read a character from the keyboard and display it on the video screen

the character colon (:) to a variable of that name, that had been previously declared to be of type char, the following expression would suffice:

```
colon := ':';
```

It is also often useful to declare character constants at the start of a program. This is done in a similar way. If, for instance, a number of characters are to be used as special symbols, the constant declarations might look like this:

```
CONST
   dollar = '$';
   period = '.';
   plus = '+';
   minus = '-';
   times = '*';
   divide = '/';
   equals = '=';
```

It is necessary, because of PASCAL's strong rules against mixing data types, to use special type conversion functions when obtaining the integer representation of the character code, or obtaining the character represented by a particular character code. These are the standard functions 'ord' and 'chr'. So that where i is declared to be an integer, and ch is declared to be of type char:

```
i  := ord(ch);
```

places the integer equivalent of the character held in ch in i. The opposite conversion is obtained with the standard function 'chr', so that:

```
ch := chr(i);
```

places the character whose ASCII code is held in i, in ch.

It is therefore possible to write a program that displays the ASCII code for any key on the keyboard (program 4.9).

```
PROGRAM convertchar(input,output);

VAR
   ch : char;

BEGIN
   page(output);
   writeln;
   write('TYPE IN ANY CHARACTER -->');
   read(ch);
   writeln;
   writeln;
   writeln('THE CODE FOR ',ch,' IS ',ord(ch))
END.
```

Program 4.9 A program to read a character from the keyboard and display the ASCII character code

4.9 PROBLEMS

4.1 Calculate the value assigned to the integer variable on the left of each of the following assignment statements. Assume each statement is executed in sequence:

```
a := 20;
b := a-10;
```

```
c := a DIV b;
d := a MOD (c+1);
e := a*(c+1);
f := a*c+1;
```

4.2 Write type declarations that would be suitable for the following data items:

(a) A set of marks, in the range 0 to 100.
(b) The vowels, A, E, I, O and U.

4.3 It is intended to run a program on a microcomputer which allows integers to take values between -128 and +127. It is necessary to test this program on a microcomputer whose PASCAL compiler allows integers to take values over a far wider range. Write the declarations that would be needed to test the program adequately on the larger system, and allow it to be transferred to the first system with the minimum of modification, apart from recompilation.

4.4 Write a program to read two integers in from the keyboard, and to display the number of times that the second may be divided into the first, and the remainder.

4.5 Write a program that will convert a length, entered in yards, feet and inches, into metres.

4.6 Write a program which, after reading an amount, the rate of interest, and the number of years invested, will calculate the simple interest payable.

4.7 Write a program which will convert a distance quoted in kilometres into miles and yards.

CHAPTER 5

Telling the Computer to Make Decisions

5.1 INTRODUCTION

So far, in all the programs that have been looked at, each program statement has been executed in turn, starting with the statement immediately after BEGIN, and continuing until the end of the program is reached. In other words, all the programs that have been considered so far have been executed sequentially. While many very useful and worthwhile programs can be written in this way, many more problems can be solved if the microcomputer can be programmed to execute different sections of code depending on the value of the available data. If, in addition, the microcomputer can be told to execute certain sections of code many times, the basis will have been laid for programming most data-processing applications.

As was shown in Chapter 2, programs of this sort can be written very easily. The different control structures associated with structured programming were introduced, including the sequence, the condition, and the loop. It is the intention of this chapter to look at how conditions are programmed in PASCAL, and how programs may be written to solve some of the problems that require the use of them. Chapter 6 looks at the different ways of programming loops in PASCAL. With these two additional capabilities, it will be possible to write programs to perform all of the operations that are required to solve both data processing and computational problems.

5.2 THE SIMPLE CONDITION

Many problems require the microcomputer to take some action only if certain conditions are met. This is simply programmed using an IF clause of the following type:

```
IF <condition> THEN
     <statement>;
```

where the condition may be a logical expression, or more likely, a relational expression which returns the value TRUE or FALSE. In this way the values held in variables may be compared, and the desired action taken. The body of the condition is only executed if the condition is found to be true.

To compare the value held in a variable, it is necessary to use special operators called relational operators. These have the effect of comparing the value of two arithmetic expressions, and returning the value TRUE, if the condition is met, and FALSE, otherwise. The relational operators that are available in PASCAL are as follows:

<	less than
<=	less than, or equal to
=	equal to
>=	greater than, or equal to
>	greater than

so that if, for example the programmer wishes to test some value stored in inputvalue to see whether it is less than zero, and to print an error message if it is, he would write:

```
IF inputvalue < 0 THEN
   writeln('error - value less than zero');
```

If a number of conditions must be satisfied, before a section of code can be executed, the boolean operators:

NOT
AND
and OR

can be very useful. If for instance the programmer wishes to warn the user that values of i outside the range 0 to 99 are invalid he can write:

```
IF i<0 OR i>99 THEN
   writeln ('i = ',i,' is invalid');
```

or, if the only characters that he wishes ch (which he has declared to be of type CHAR) to contain are 'a', 'e', 'i', 'o' and 'u', then he could write:

```
IF NOT (ch='a' OR ch='e' OR ch='i' OR ch='o' OR ch='u') THEN
    writeln(ch,' is an invalid input character');
```

In expressions which mix arithmetic, relational and boolean operators, it is important to ensure that they are executed in the desired order. In PASCAL, the arithmetic operators are evaluated first, followed by the relational operators, and then the logical operators, thus following the normal rules of mathematics. Operators of the same priority are executed, in order, from left to right.

```
PROGRAM metric(input,output);

CONST
   factor = 39.37;   (* THE NUMBER OF INCHES IN
                        ONE METRE.*)
VAR
   metres : real;
   inches,feet,yards  : integer;

BEGIN
   page(output);
   writeln;
   writeln;
   writeln('A PROGRAM TO CONVERT FROM METRES, TO');
   writeln('YARDS, FEET AND INCHES.');
   writeln;
   writeln;
   write('ENTER THE LENGTH IN METRES -->');
   readln(metres);
   metres := abs(metres);
   inches := round(factor*metres);
   feet := inches DIV 12;
   inches := inches MOD 12;
   yards := feet DIV 3;
   feet := feet MOD 3;
```

```
        writeln;
        writeln;
        writeln;
        writeln(metres,' METRES,  IS EQUIVALENT TO');
        IF yards > 0 THEN
           write(yards,' YARDS, ');
        IF feet > 0 THEN
           write(feet,' FEET, ');
        IF (yards >0) OR (feet>0) THEN
           write('AND ');
        writeln(inches,' INCHES.')
     END.
```

Program 5.1 A program to convert from metres to yards, feet and inches

Program 5.1 is an expansion of the unit conversion programs discussed in the last chapter. In the simple form of these programs, all the units are displayed, even if the number in the conversion is zero. This looks silly, and may well confuse the naive user. Simple conditions may be used to remove those which have values of zero. In addition, the standard function abs is used to ensure that the conversion algorithm works successfully, even if the user enters a negative length.

5.3 SELECTING ONE OF TWO DIFFERENT WAYS

In many problems, the need is to perform one set of operations if some condition is met, and another if not. For this a single condition is insufficient. PASCAL, therefore, provides another conditional construction of the form:

```
IF <condition> THEN
     <statement>
ELSE
     <statement>
```

in which the first statement is executed as long as the condition is met, otherwise the second statement is used. This is a very powerful construction which is used frequently in most programs.

```
PROGRAM oddoreven(input,output);

VAR
  num : integer;
  test : 0..1;

BEGIN
   page(output);
   writeln;
   writeln;
   writeln('A PROGRAM TO TEST WHETHER A NUMBER IS ODD OR EVEN');
   writeln;
   writeln;
   writeln;
   write('ENTER THE NUMBER -->');
   readln(num);
   test := num MOD 2;
   writeln;
   writeln;
   writeln;
   write(num,' IS ');
   IF test=0 THEN
      writeln('EVEN.')
   ELSE
      writeln('ODD.')
END.
```

Program 5.2 A program to read in an integer from the keyboard, and to display whether it is an even number, or not

In the first example, program 5.2, the IF ... THEN ... ELSE construction is used to determine whether an integer is odd or even by taking the number modulus 2. If this is zero, the number is even, otherwise it is odd. The condition is used to display the word ODD or EVEN, as appropriate.

Another use is to allow the user to choose between two different execution paths. Program 5.3 shows how this can be done. The program can be used to calculate either the area or the circumference of a circle. First the radius must be entered by the user. Since this will be needed for both calculations, the data entry part of the program is common to both paths. Once the radius has been entered, the program asks the user whether the area or the circumference is

```
PROGRAM circle2(input,output);

CONST
   pi = 3.1416;

VAR
   radius,answer : real;
   ch : char;

BEGIN
   page(output);
   writeln;
   writeln('A PROGRAM TO CALCULATE THE AREA OR THE');
   writeln('CIRCUMFERENCE OF A CIRCLE');
   writeln;
   writeln;
   write('WHAT IS THE RADIUS OF THE CIRCLE IN CM? -->');
   readln(radius);
   writeln;
   writeln;
   write('A(REA OR C(IRCUMFERENCE -->');
   read(ch);
   writeln;
   writeln;
   writeln;
   IF ch = 'A' THEN
      BEGIN
         answer := pi*sqr(radius);
         writeln('THE AREA IS ',answer,' SQ CM.')
      END
   ELSE
      IF ch = 'C' THEN
         BEGIN
            answer := 2*pi*radius;
            writeln('THE CIRCUMFERENCE IS ',answer,' CM.')
         END
      ELSE
         writeln('THIS OPTION IS NOT AVAILABLE.')
END.
```

Program 5.3 A program to calculate the area or circumference of a circle required. Once he has replied, the answer is calculated, and displayed, as one or other branch of the condition.

5.4 THE COMPOUND STATEMENT

In many cases, one PASCAL statement is insufficient to program the action that is required when the condition is met. PASCAL provides a method of collecting a series of program statements together, called a compound statement. This allows the programmer to bracket a whole sequence of instructions, to be executed only if certain conditions are met. This is done by enclosing them with the keywords BEGIN and, END, in this way:

```
IF <condition> THEN
   BEGIN
      <a series of program statements>
   END
ELSE
   BEGIN
      <another series of program statements>
   END;
```

For instance, if it was desired to trap a negative number input from the keyboard, display a message to say that an input error has been detected, and change the number to zero, the following section of code would suffice:

```
       .
       .
       .
    VAR
        i : integer;
       .
       .
       .
       write('enter a number greater than zero -->');
       readln(i);
       IF i<0 THEN
          BEGIN
              writeln(i,' is less than 0, 0 substituted');
              i:=0
          END;
```

As an example of how compound statements can be used to develop complex programs where it is necessary to execute several statements along each branch of the condition, program 5.4 calculates the date of Easter, using one of the available formulae. It is necessary not only to use a compound statement to calculate the date, if it falls in March, but also a number of nested conditions to determine on which day in April it will fall.

```
PROGRAM easter(input,output);

VAR
   year:integer;
   a,b,c,d,e,day,t:integer;

BEGIN
   page(output);
   writeln('THIS PROGRAM CALCULATES THE DATE OF');
   writeln;
   writeln('EASTER WHEN GIVEN A YEAR');
   writeln;
   writeln;
   write('FOR WHAT YEAR ? -->');
   readln(year);
   IF year<99 THEN
      year:=year+1900;
   b:=year MOD 4;
   c:=year MOD 7;
   t:=19*(year MOD 19)+24;
   d:=t MOD 30;
   t:= 2*b+4*c+6*d+5;
   day:=d+(t MOD 7)-9;
   IF day<0 THEN
      BEGIN
         day:=day+31;
         writeln('EASTER FALLS ON MARCH ',day,' ',year)
      END
   ELSE
      IF day=26 THEN
         writeln('EASTER FALLS ON APRIL 19, ',year)
```

```
          ELSE
             IF (day=25) AND (d=28) THEN
                writeln('EASTER FALLS ON APRIL 18,  ',year)
             ELSE
                writeln('EASTER FALLS ON APRIL ',day,',',year);
   END.
```

Program 5.4 A program to calculate the date of Easter in any given year

5.5 SELECTING ONE OF SEVERAL POSSIBILITIES

While most problems can be broken down into a series of single- or double-branched IF statements, it is sometimes necessary to select one of a whole series of possible actions, dependent on the value of some variable. This can be done most easily using a CASE statement of the following form:

```
CASE <variable> OF
     <value1> : <statement 1>;
     <value2> : <statement 2>;
     <value3> : <statement 3>;
     <value4> : <statement 4>;
     <value5> : <statement 5>
END;
```

where <value1>, <value2> etc. are allowed values of <variable>. For example, if ch is declared of type CHAR, and can contain one of the characters +, -, * or /, then the following section of code will print the name of the relevant operator:

```
CASE ch OF
   '+' : writeln('plus');
   '-' : writeln('minus');
   '*' : writeln('times');
   '/' : writeln('divide')
END;
```

In standard PASCAL, <variable> can only take the values listed in the body of the CASE statement. An execution error would therefore result from any attempt to execute the CASE statement if this variable contained any other variable than those listed. It is therefore necessary for the programmer to ensure that adequate checks are made to ensure that this does not happen.

Program 5.5 uses a case statement to convert a hexadecimal digit (i.e. one of the characters '0' to '9', or 'a' to 'f', representing a number from 0_{10} to 15_{10}) into its decimal eqivalent. This is particularily clumsy in this case, and other methods of performing the same operation will be discussed in a later chapter, but it is perfectly workable, and gives a very good illustration of the operation of the CASE statement.

```
PROGRAM hexdigit(input,output);

VAR
   ch : char;
   num: integer;

BEGIN
   page(output);
   writeln;
   writeln;
   write('ENTER A HEXADECIMAL DIGIT -->');
   read(ch);
   writeln;
   writeln;
   CASE ch OF
        '0' : num:=0;
        '1' : num:=1;
        '2' : num:=2;
        '3' : num:=3;
        '4' : num:=4;
        '5' : num:=5;
        '6' : num:=6;
        '7' : num:=7;
        '8' : num:=8;
        '9' : num:=9;
        'A' : num:=10;
        'B' : num:=11;
        'C' : num:=12;
        'D' : num:=13;
        'E' : num:=14;
        'F' : num:=15
   END;
```

```
   writeln(num,' IS THE DECIMAL EQIVALENT OF ',ch)
END.
```

Program 5.5 A program to accept a hexadecimal digit typed in from the keyboard, and to display the decimal equivalent on the display

One very common use of CASE statements is to select one of a number of different options displayed on the screen. These are selected, simply, by pressing one of a series of keys depending on what action it is intended that the microcomputer should take. This is, in essence, a simple menu, which allows the operator to select one of a number of different options, without knowing anything about the structure of the program, or how it is written. As the program is written, the user must take care to ensure that an allowable option is selected, since otherwise an execution error will result. For a program in general use, this is undesireable, because it does not say what is wrong. Checks must therefore be included, as will be seen later.

```
PROGRAM printer(input,output);

VAR
  ch    : char;

BEGIN
  page(output);
  writeln;
  writeln;
  writeln('PRINTER OPTION SELECTION PROGRAM.');
  writeln;
  writeln;
  writeln;
  writeln('OPTIONS AVAILABLE');
  writeln;
  writeln('  A.   132 CHARACTERS PER LINE');
  writeln;
  writeln('  B.    80 CHARACTERS PER LINE');
  writeln;
  writeln('  C.    40 CHARACTERS PER LINE');
```

```
    writeln;
    writeln;
    write('ENTER OPTION SELECTED -->');
    read(ch);
    CASE ch OF
       'A' : write(chr(29));
       'B' : write(chr(30));
       'C' : write(chr(31));
    END
  END.
```

Program 5.6 A program to change the number of characters displayed on each line of the principal output device, using the character codes discussed in the text

For example, program 5.6 shows how a program can be written to control an output device, such as a printer that requires special codes to tell it how many characters to display on each line. When the program is run, a menu is first displayed, to tell the user what the program does, and the options that are available. The operator then selects which one he requires, and presses the key as requested. A CASE statement is then used to send the right characters to the display device to make it operate in the desired mode.

In this case, the number of characters per line is selected by sending the ASCII characters represented by the following codes:

	29	for 40 characters per line
	30	for 80 characters per line
and	31	for 132 characters per line

Once the characters have been sent, the program terminates immediately, since it is unlikely that the user is going to want to change the character spacing again. If he presses the wrong key, he can correct the error by simply rerunning the program from scratch.

With simple menus such as this, it is possible to test the input to ensure that the option selected is valid with IF statements immediately before the CASE. This is done in program 5.7, making this a much more usable program for someone other than the original programmer. If a key is pressed that does not correspond to a valid option, a message to this effect is displayed, and the program terminates. In the next chapter it will be seen how the menu can be displayed again, and the user asked to retype his reply.

```
PROGRAM printer(input,output);

VAR
  ch    : char;

BEGIN
  page(output);
  writeln;
  writeln;
  writeln('PRINTER OPTION SELECTION PROGRAM.');
  writeln;
  writeln;
  writeln;
  writeln('OPTIONS AVAILABLE');
  writeln;
  writeln('  A.   132 CHARACTERS PER LINE');
  writeln;
  writeln('  B.    80 CHARACTERS PER LINE');
  writeln;
  writeln('  C.    40 CHARACTERS PER LINE');
  writeln;
  writeln;
  write('ENTER OPTION SELECTED -->');
  read(ch);
  IF (ch='A') OR (ch='B') OR (ch='C') THEN
     CASE ch OF
        'A' : write(chr(29));
        'B' : write(chr(30));
        'C' : write(chr(31));
     END
  ELSE
     BEGIN
        writeln;
        writeln;
        writeln('THIS IS NOT AN ALLOWABLE OPTION')
     END
END.
```

Program 5.7 Another version of program 5.6 which checks the option selected to see that it is valid

Program 5.8 is another menu-driven program. In this case, the object is to convert angles given in degrees to radians, or if they are already in radians, to convert them into degrees. Two case statements are used, one to select which of the conversions is required, and the other to print the units after the answer.

```
PROGRAM angles1(input,output);

CONST
    pi=3.1416;

VAR
    ch:char;
    angle:real;

BEGIN
    page(output);
    writeln;
    writeln;
    writeln('A PROGRAM TO CONVERT ANGLES');
    writeln('= ======= == ======= ======');
    writeln;
    writeln;
    writeln('CONVERT TO RADIANS (R)');
    writeln;
    writeln('     OR TO DEGREES (D)');
    writeln;
    write('WHICH CHOICE ? -->');
    read(ch);
    writeln;
    writeln;
    write('ANGLE TO BE CONVERTED -->');
    readln(angle);
    CASE ch OF
       'D'  :  angle := (angle/pi)*180.0;
       'R'  :  angle := (angle*pi)/180.0
    END;
    writeln;
    write('THE ANGLE IS ?',angle,' ');
```

```
    CASE ch OF
       'D' : writeln('DEGREES');
       'R' : writeln('RADIANS');
    END;
    writeln
END.
```

Program 5.8 A program to convert angles from degrees to radians, or from radians to degrees

5.6 PROBLEMS

5.1 Write a program that will display a message if, and only if, an integer typed in from the keyboard is an odd number.

5.2 Write a program that will display a message to say whether, or not, a number typed in from the keyboard is exactly divisible by four.

5.3 Write a program to determine which of two numbers entered from the keyboard is the smaller.

5.4 Write a program that displays one of the following messages, if the appropriate key is pressed.

key	message
a	the first message
b	the second message
c	the third message
d	the fourth message
e	the last message.

5.5 Write a program which will display the number, in words, of the digit key pressed on the keyboard, i.e. when 0 is pressed, the program will display ZERO, etc.

5.6 Write a program to calculate the area of a triangle, a square or a circle, depending on which option the user selects.

5.7 Write a program to read in a number and print out its square root (remember to check that the number read is positive).

CHAPTER 6
Writing Programs to Perform Repetitive Calculations

6.1 INTRODUCTION

So far, ways in which the computer can be programmed to perform a number of different types of calculation have been looked at. Apart from the memory size, and the wide range of peripherals available on most computers, these calculations could be done perfectly adequately on most modern programmable pocket calculators. Where the computer is of most benefit is when a particular calculation must be repeated many times, either to form some sort of iterative solution, or on a large number of different sets of data. It is then necessary to program loops, in which certain sequences of operations are performed many times, something which can usually be done only very clumsily on most programmable calculators, and would invariably execute very slowly. It is here that the computer's power is most prominent, since it is able to execute many thousands of program steps every second.

It is well worth while spending some time considering the best way to program code which is included within a loop. If more instructions than are absolutely necessary are executed in a part of the program which is used only once, very little time will be lost, whereas if they are in a loop which is executed say a thousand times, a great deal of computer time can be wasted. In many applications this may not be of any great importance, but if the computer is expected to respond to some outside stimulus, or the program is of any great complexity, and the user is sitting waiting for the computer to finish, speed is of the essence. It is therefore essential to have clear ways of programming loops, which are obvious to the programmer, and anyone else who wishes to read his program subsequently. It is then much easier to recognise those parts of the code which must be executed every time the loop is entered, and those which can be safely kept outside, and thus executed only once.

In PASCAL, there are several ways of programming a control loop, each of which operates in a slightly different way. This allows the programmer to choose the most appropriate form for the algorithm he intends to use. This choice can depend on a number of different factors, but is usually made on the basis of the precise conditions that must be met before the execution of the loop can be terminated. These conditions must be determined very carefully, since if under any circumstances they cannot be met, the computer will continue to perform the operations programmed within the loop for ever, with possibly disastrous consequences, or at least to the considerable annoyance of whoever is trying to use the program.

If it is intended that the loop is to be executed so long as some condition still exists, the WHILE construction is appropriate.

```
WHILE <some condition is met> DO
    <statement>
```

If, however, the loop is to be executed until some condition is met the REPEAT construction can be used.

```
REPEAT
    <statement>
UNTIL <some condition is met>
```

Essentially the difference between a WHILE loop and a REPEAT loop is that in a WHILE loop the test, as to whether the terminating condition is met, takes place at the start of the loop, and therefore if it is met before the WHILE statement is executed the code within the loop will never be used, whereas in the case of the REPEAT loop the test takes place at the end of the loop, and the code within the loop will always be executed at least once.

It is often the case that the programmer knows exactly how many times a certain group of statements must be executed to obtain the required result. This is particularily true when tables are to be printed, and in other situations where the data available is fixed. PASCAL provides the FOR loop construction for this situation. A special variable, called a control variable, is programmed to take values on successive executions of the loop which are between the lower and upper limits specified. The control variable, which must be declared as an integer or a scalar, is set to the starting value the first time the statements within the loop are executed, and is incremented by one until the finishing value is reached.

```
FOR <control variable> := <starting value> TO <finishing value> DO
     <statement>
```

If the control variable is to be decremented (that is the starting value is greater than the finishing value) then DOWNTO is used rather than TO.

```
FOR <control variable> := <starting value>
     DOWNTO <finishing value> DO
      <statement>
```

In PASCAL the control variable can only be incremented, or decremented, by one each time the loop is executed. If some other value is required the programmer must include suitable code within the loop. This may, at first, appear a little strange to the inexperienced programmer, but is, in fact, how the computer has to perform this sort of loop, even if it is allowed within the language.

6.2 THE 'WHILE' LOOP

Probably the simplest of PASCAL's loop constructions to understand is the WHILE loop, in which the condition for execution of the loop is tested at the beginning. The loop is executed so long as the condition coded within the WHILE clause is true. The WHILE clause can be followed by any simple, or compound, statement to be executed as the body of the loop. Since the terminating condition is tested at the start of the loop, the loop is not entered when this condition is evaluated as false, and the body of the loop is not executed at all.

Typical of the applications where WHILE loops are most useful are programs which evaluate an expression as the sum of a converging arithmetic series. This is a very convenient way of calculating the value of a wide range of arithmetic functions, for which it is impracticable to store all the possible values as tables in the computer's memory.

Program 6.1 evaluates the value of the series

$$f(x) = 1/1 + 1/2 + 1/3 + 1/4 + \ldots$$

until the value of the next term is less than some error factor, 'epsilon'.

```
PROGRAM series(input,output);

CONST
    epsilon = 0.01;

VAR
    term:real;
    sum :real;
    n   :real;

BEGIN
    sum :=0;
    n :=1;
    term:=1;
    WHILE term>epsilon DO
    BEGIN
       term:=1/n;
       sum:=sum+term;
       n:=n+1
    END;
    writeln('THE SUM OF THIS SERIES IS ',sum)
END.
```

Program 6.1 Program to calculate the sum of a simple arithmetic series

This is not a particularly useful series, but there are many that are. For instance e^x can be evaluated as

e^x = 1 + x + x^2/2! + x^3/3! ... for all x.

(n! is the product 1 * 2 * 3 * ... * n-1 * n, and is known as the factorial of n, where n is a positive integer.) Program 6.2 evaluates e^x following the same principles as program 6.1. To write the program it is necessary to determine how the series repeats, and to code this within the loop.

```
PROGRAM power(input,output);

CONST
    epsilon = 0.0001;

VAR
    x       :real;
    xpower  :real;
    term    :real;
    sum     :real;
    n       :real;
    fact    :real;

BEGIN
    sum :=1.0;
    n :=1.0;
    term:=1.0;
    fact:=1.0;
    write('ENTER VALUE OF X --> ');
    readln(x);
    xpower:=x;
    WHILE term>epsilon DO
    BEGIN
       term:=xpower/fact;
       sum:=sum+term;
       xpower:=x*xpower;
       n:=n+1.0;
       fact:=n*fact
    END;
    writeln('E^X IS ',sum)
END.
```

Program 6.2 A program to calculate the value of e^x using the arithmetic series

Another reason for needing to make the program enter a loop is when the problem requires a series of data items to be entered. Program 6.3 is an example of this type of application. Resistors can be connected in parallel (figure 6.1), and the total resistance is given by the formula

$$1/R = 1/R_1 + 1/R_2 + 1/R_3 + \ldots$$

where R, R_1, etc. are given in ohms. Since any number of resistors

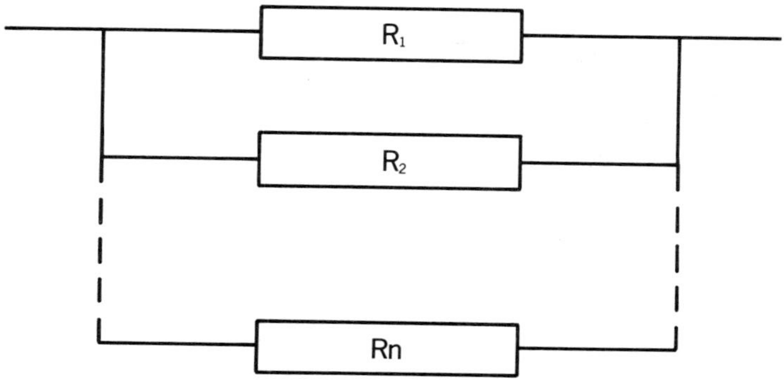

Figure 6.1 Resistors connected in parallel

can be used, it is necessary to define some way in which the user can tell the program that all the data has been entered. As no useful function can be served with a resistor of value 0 ohms, and indeed it would cause an arithmetic error since the value of 1/0 is undefined, this is a suitable input to signal the end of the data.

```
PROGRAM resistance(input,output);

(*  A PROGRAM TO CALCULATE THE TOTAL VALUE OF A NUMBER OF
    RESISTORS CONNECTED IN PARALLEL.                        *)

VAR
   resistor:integer;
   totalres:real;

BEGIN
    totalres:=0.0;
    writeln('TO FINISH, ENTER A RESISTOR VALUE OF');
    writeln('            ZERO, OR A NEGATIVE VALUE');
```

```
        writeln;
        write('ENTER FIRST RESISTOR VALUE -->');
        readln(resistor);
        WHILE resistor>0 DO
        BEGIN
            totalres:=totalres+1.0/resistor;
            write('ENTER NEXT RESISTOR VALUE -->');
            readln(resistor)
        END;
        totalres:=1.0/totalres;
        writeln;
        writeln('THE TOTAL RESISTANCE IS ',totalres)
    END.
```

Program 6.3 A program to calculate the total resistance of a number of resistors connected in parallel

6.3 THE 'REPEAT' LOOP

The REPEAT loop construction performs a very similar function to the WHILE loop construction. The difference is that the test to determine whether the loop is to be executed again is made at the end of the

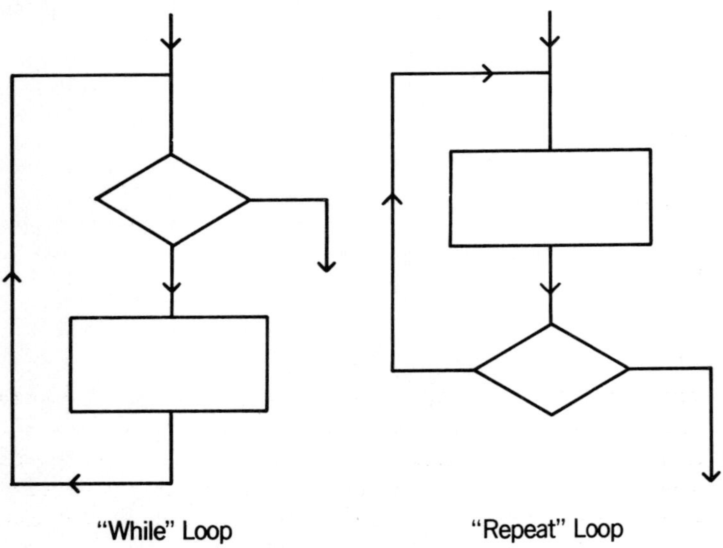

Figure 6.2 Flow diagrams showing where the terminating condition is checked in WHILE and REPEAT loops

loop, rather than the beginning (as in figure 6.2). This is particularly useful in many applications, including commercial, scientific and systems programming.

It is often the case that a series of statements is to be executed until some terminating condition is met. This is very easily programmed in PASCAL by declaring a boolean variable called, for instance, FINISHED, and setting it to FALSE before the start of the loop. Once the terminating condition is met, FINISHED is set to TRUE and the program exits at the end of the loop. The code to do this will look something like

```
PROGRAM repeated(input,output);

   <declarations>

VAR
   finished:boolean;

BEGIN

    <initialisation statements>

   finished:=false;
   REPEAT
       <processing statements>
      IF <terminating condition is met> THEN
        finished:=true;
       <more processing statements>
   UNTIL finished;

    <terminating statements>

END.
```

This can be illustrated by program 6.4, which is designed to add numbers entered into the computer until either zero, or a negative number, is encountered, when the total of those numbers already entered is printed, and the program terminates. The simpler solution of simply checking for a zero, or negative number in the UNTIL clause cannot be used, since if the program was to terminate after reading a negative number rather than zero, the resultant sum would be incorrect unless some very messy, and somewhat obscure, code was added to correct it.

```
PROGRAM sumprog(input,output);

VAR
   number:real;
   sum    :real;
   finished:boolean;

BEGIN
   sum:=0.0;
   finished:=false;
   REPEAT
      write('ENTER NUMBER -->');
      readln(number);
      IF number<=0.0 THEN
         finished:=true
      ELSE
         sum:=sum+number
   UNTIL finished;
   writeln('THE SUM IS ',sum)
END.
```

Program 6.4 Program to form the sum of a series of numbers terminated by zero, or a negative number

Of course if the loop is to be executed indefinitely the code necessary is greatly diminished. It is only necessary to test for the impossible situation of FALSE being TRUE to ensure that the loop is executed continually.
For instance,

```
PROGRAM forever(input,output);

    <declarations>

BEGIN
    <initialisation statements>
   REPEAT
      <processing statements>
   UNTIL false
END.
```

If this code is used and the program is expected to terminate, some other exit path must be provided, for instance by calling another program, if this is allowed on your system. In many systems and production control programs this is unnecessary as they are designed to run all the time that the computer is in use.

Another use of the REPEAT statment is to provide a choice of options at the end of an operation. For instance, to ask the user if he wishes to perform the operation again, the following code would suffice

```
PROGRAM answer(input,answer);

   <declarations>

VAR
   ch:char;

BEGIN
     <initialisation statements>
   REPEAT
         <processing statements>
      write('another problem y(es or n(o');
      read(ch);
      writeln;
   UNTIL ch='y';
     <terminating statements>
END.
```

This code means that the code within the loop will be executed until the prompt is answered by pressing the 'y' key. The rest of the program is then run.

This is illustrated by program 6.5, which finds the roots of quadratic equations of the form

$$a*x^2 + b*x + c = 0$$

and uses this to allow the user to solve more than one equation without having to rerun the program. Within the loop, the user is first asked for the parameters a,b and c. The roots are then found using the equation

$$x = \frac{-b \pm \sqrt{(b^2 - 4*a*c)}}{2*a}$$

The three possible solutions, of there being two real roots, only one real root, and two complex roots, are determined once the value of (b^2 - 4*a*c) (on which the appropriate solution depends) has been calculated by the two nested IF statements. If the value of this part of the equation is zero there is only one root. So long as it is positive there are two real roots, otherwise there are two complex roots. The program handles all three situations.

```
PROGRAM quadratic(input,output);

VAR
   a,b,c : real;
   root1,root2 : real;
   sroot : real;
   ch : char;

BEGIN
    REPEAT
       page(output);
       writeln;
       writeln('PROGRAM TO FIND THE ROOTS OF A QUADRATIC');
       writeln;
       writeln('         EQUATION OF THE FORM');
       writeln;
       writeln;
       writeln('          A*X^2 + B*X + C =0');
       writeln;
       writeln;
       write('ENTER A -->');
       readln(a);
       write('ENTER B -->');
       readln(b);
       write('ENTER C -->');
       readln(c);
       writeln;
    IF a=0.0 THEN
          BEGIN
             writeln('THIS EQUATION IS LINEAR, NOT QUADRATIC');
             root1 := -c/b;
             writeln('ITS ROOT IS ',root1)
          END
```

```
        ELSE
           BEGIN
              sroot:=sqr(b)-4.0*a*c;
              IF sroot=0.0 THEN
                  BEGIN
                     root1:=-b/(2.0*a);
                     writeln('THERE IS ONLY ONE REAL ROOT,');
                     writeln;
                     writeln('AND IT IS  - ',root1)
                  END
              ELSE
                  IF sroot>0.0 THEN
                      BEGIN
                         sroot:=sqrt(sroot);
                         root1:=(-b+sroot)/(2*a);
                         root2:=(-b-sroot)/(2*a);
                         writeln('THERE ARE TWO REAL ROOTS,');
                         writeln;
                         writeln('AND THEY ARE - ',root1,
                                ' AND ',root2)
                      END
                  ELSE
                      BEGIN
                         sroot:=sqrt(abs(sroot));
                         root1:=-b/(2*a);
                         root2:=sroot/(2*a);
                         write('THERE ARE TWO IMAGINARY ROOTS,');
                         writeln;
                         writeln('AND THEY ARE - ',root1,
                                ' + OR - ',root2)
                      END
        END;
        writeln;
        write('ANOTHER PROBLEM ? Y(ES OR N(O -->');
        read(ch);
        writeln
     UNTIL ch<>'Y'
  END.
```

Program 6.5 A program to find the roots of a quadratic equation

6.4 LOOPING A SET NUMBER OF TIMES

It is sometimes the case that the programmer knows how many times the loop is to be executed when he writes the program, or he may wish to enter this at the start of the data. PASCAL provides a special form of the loop which automatically provides a count of the number of times it has been executed. This is in the form of the FOR statement. The programmer is accorded considerable flexibility by the ability to specify initial and final values between which the loop counter can be either incremented or decremented.

One of the traditional uses of the FOR statement has been to read in a sequence of known length before calculating some result. The program can be made for general use by reading in the number of items to be processed at the start of the program. Program 6.6, which is intended to calculate the mean of a set of data, illustrates this. It soon becomes apparent, however, that it is very inconvenient to have to count the data items before entering them into the computer. This is a job the computer is far better at than most human operators. Also the user will not necessarily know how many items he wishes to enter until much later. It is usually more appropriate to ask the user to mark the end of the data with some special value, as in program 6.4.

```
PROGRAM averageprog(input,output);

VAR
   number:integer;
   i     :integer;
   value,total,average:real;

BEGIN
   total:=0.0;
   write('HOW MANY NUMBERS ? --> ');
   readln(number);
   FOR i:= 1 TO number DO
   BEGIN
      write('NEXT VALUE -->');
      readln(value);
      total:=total+value
   END;
```

```
    writeln('THE TOTAL IS ',total);
    average:=total/number;
    writeln('AND THE AVERAGE IS ',average)
END.
```

Program 6.6 A program to calculate the mean of a series of numbers

If the program is to print out a set of tables, the FOR loop is highly appropriate. Program 6.7 is an example of this. The object is to calculate the square roots of the numbers between one and ten. Since all the values required are integers, no special scaling within the loop is required. The loop counter is taken as the number whose root is to be found, and is printed each time round. The table is built up by printing the result of each calculation under the last, until all the required results are generated.

```
PROGRAM root1(input,output);

CONST
     first=1;
     last =10;

VAR
   i:integer;
   sqroot:real;

BEGIN
   FOR i:= first TO last DO
   BEGIN
      sqroot:=sqrt(i);
      writeln(i,'  ',sqroot)
   END
END.
```

Program 6.7 A program to calculate the square roots of the numbers from 1 to 10

This is fine so long as the user only wants to generate tables for functions whose arguments are always whole numbers. In reality this is rarely very useful. Program 6.8 is an example of how the last program can be extended to allow square roots of real numbers other than integers to be calculated.

```
PROGRAM root2(input,output);

CONST
     first=0;
     last =9;
     base=1;
     increment=0.1;

VAR
   i:integer;
   value,sqroot:real;

BEGIN
   FOR i:= first TO last DO
   BEGIN
      value:=base+i*increment;
      sqroot:=sqrt(value);
      writeln(value,'  ',sqroot)
   END
END.
```

Program 6.8 A program to calculate the square roots of numbers from 1.0 to 2.0

In this case the object is to calculate square roots of real numbers from one to two, in steps of 0.1. A special variable called VALUE is declared, and it is recalculated each time round the loop. This is the value whose square root is to form the next entry in the table, and is formed from the loop counter. By choosing suitable constants the square root can then be calculated over any range, at any desired frequency.

6.5 PROBLEMS

6.1 Write a program to read a set of student marks, and print out the number of passes and fails. Assume the pass mark is 35%.

6.2 Rewrite program 5.5 so that if the user presses an undefined key, the menu is redisplayed, and he is invited to try again.

6.3 Write a program to read a series of numbers, finishing with a zero, and display the smallest positive value.

6.4 Write a program to read a series of numbers, finishing with a zero, and display the largest and smallest.

6.5 Write a program to see how many even numbers must be added together before the sum is greater than 100.

6.6 Write a filter program that calculates the average of a series of numbers entered from the keyboard. The maximum and the minimum values to be accepted should be entered before processing commences. The average, together with the number of data items accepted and rejected, should be displayed at the end of the program.

CHAPTER 7

Breaking the Program Up Into Manageable Sections

7.1 THE NEED FOR PROCEDURES

Not very many programs that are written to solve real problems are likely to be as simple and straightforward as those discussed so far. In most cases they will perform a number of separate tasks which are logically distinct. If these sections can be programmed independently, the task of developing a program can be greatly eased. Most programmers can remain sufficiently familiar with only a limited amount of code to develop it satisfactorily. This is usually in the range of fifty to sixty lines in any programming language, or in other words approximately the amount that can be printed on one page. In PASCAL, procedures are used to break the program up into its various sub-tasks.

It is often necessary to perform the same task in several different places within the program. It would be wasteful of both memory and programming resources to repeat the same code at each of these points. However, it is possible to invoke a separate procedure to perform the required task, wherever it is needed. The amount of code required to do this is quite small, so that if there are more than a very few instructions within the procedure, the saving on the memory required to store the object code to run the program is quite considerable.

The procedure, of course, need be developed only once, no matter how many times it is called and run. If it is to be called in many places, or can be made use of in more than one program, there is also a considerable saving in programming effort. Since the programmer always lacks sufficient time to develop adequate programs, much time and effort can be saved if those parts of the programs that are required over and over again can be developed only once, and stored away on backing store, so that they are readily accessible, whenever they are needed. It is possible to store these procedures as text, and edit them into the program before it is compiled. Most commercially available PASCAL programming systems allow the user to compile these procedures once, and store the object code on disk, from where it is included within any program that requires it. This has the considerable advantage that if the procedure needs to be rewritten, for instance, if a bug is found, only one copy need be updated, and as soon as all the programs that use it are recompiled, they will automatically include a copy of the new version.

7.2 WRITING, AND USING PROCEDURES

As with all other programmer-defined structures in PASCAL, procedures must be declared before they can be used. The definition must include, not only the code that is to be executed when the procedure is called, but also the name, or identifier, that the procedure is to be known by in the rest of the program, what information, if any, is to be given to it when it is called, and what, if any, is to be given back to the main program when execution of the procedure is finished and control is returned to the main program. This information is provided in the procedure heading, which is the only part that contains programming information relevant to the rest of the program. The procedure body should contain only information and code that is, although relevant to the proper action of the procedure, transparent to the rest of the system.

Procedures must therefore be declared, along with all the constants, data types, and variables, at the start of the program. In order that a procedure may perform its desired task, it is often the case that it must have knowledge of the data structures that have been declared for use in the rest of the program. Procedures are therefore declared immediately following all the constants, data types, and variables. In addition, if any procedure is to be used within another, it must be declared first.

The order of different declarations at the start of a program will look like this:

```
PROGRAM procedures (input,output);

CONST
     <constant declarations>
```

```
TYPE
     <type declarations>

VAR
     <variable declarations>

     <procedure declarations>

BEGIN

     <the main program>

END.
```

It is necessary to write a procedure in two parts. First, the procedure heading must specify how the procedure is to be called from the rest of the program. Apart from the procedure name, any parameters that are required must also be specified. The procedure body must then be written. This includes the definition of any constants, data types, variables, or other procedures that are to be used only within this procedure. Any other declarations that appear in the main program, or in outer procedures are also valid within the procedure, so long as no further declarations have been made with the same name. Declarations like this are said to be 'global' to the procedure in which it is used. Variable, and other declarations within the procedure itself, are said to be 'local' to it, since they can be used only within that procedure, and have no meaning once it has been left.

A typical procedure declaration would therefore be made up of the following parts:

```
PROCEDURE <procedure name> (<procedure parameters>);

CONST
     <constant declarations>

TYPE
     <type declarations>

VAR
     <variable declarations>

     <further procedure declarations>
```

```
BEGIN

     <the instructions that make up the procedure>

END;
```

If, for instance the programmer wishes to output three line feeds at various points within the program, the procedure 'spaces' can be defined as in program 7.1.

```
PROCEDURE spaces;

BEGIN
   writeln;
   writeln;
   writeln
END;
```

Program 7.1 The procedure 'spaces'

and it would be invoked within the program by name, in the following way:

```
    .
    .
    .
spaces;
    .
    .
    .
```

This is illustrated in program 7.2, where 'spaces' is called wherever it is necessary to space out the output.

```
PROGRAM simpleproc(input,output);

PROCEDURE spaces;

BEGIN
   writeln;
   writeln;
   writeln
END;

BEGIN
   page(output);
   spaces;
   writeln('THIS IS AN EXAMPLE OF A PROGRAM');
   spaces;
   writeln('WHICH CONTAINS CALLS TO A SIMPLE PROCEDURE')
END.
```

Program 7.2 An example of a simple procedure

One important use of procedures is to break a large and complex program into its component parts. It may be necessary, for instance, to write a program which will perform a number of different functions, each of which must be programmed separately. The main part of the program may well do nothing more than allow the user to select the function that he wishes to use, and then call a procedure to actually do the work.

```
PROGRAM volumes(input,output);

VAR
   ch : char;

PROCEDURE box;

VAR
   height,width,length,volume : real;
```

```
BEGIN
   page(output);
   writeln;
   writeln('CALCULATING THE VOLUME OF A BOX');
   writeln('=========== === ====== == = ===');
   writeln;
   writeln;
   writeln;
   write('WHAT IS ITS HEIGHT IN CM? -->');
   readln(height);
   write('WHAT IS ITS WIDTH IN CM?  -->');
   readln(width);
   write('WHAT IS ITS LENGTH IN CM? -->');
   readln(length);
   writeln;
   writeln;
   writeln;
   volume := height*width*length;
   writeln('THE VOLUME OF THE BOX IS ',
           volume,' CU. CM.')
END;


PROCEDURE cylinder;

CONST
   pi = 3.1416;

VAR
   radius,length,volume : real;

BEGIN
   page(output);
   writeln;
   writeln('CALCULATING THE VOLUME OF A CYLINDER');
   writeln('=========== === ====== == = ========');
   writeln;
   writeln;
   writeln;
   write('WHAT IS ITS RADIUS IN CM? -->');
   readln(radius);
   write('WHAT IS ITS LENGTH IN CM? -->');
   readln(length);
```

```
   writeln;
   writeln;
   writeln;
   volume := length*pi*sqr(radius);
   writeln('THE VOLUME OF THE CYLINDER IS ',
           volume,' CU. CM.')
END;


PROCEDURE kone;

CONST
   pi = 3.1416;

VAR
   radius,length,volume : real;

BEGIN
   page(output);
   writeln;
   writeln('CALCULATING THE VOLUME OF A CONE');
   writeln('=========== === ====== == = ====');
   writeln;
   writeln;
   writeln;
   write('WHAT IS ITS RADIUS IN CM? -->');
   readln(radius);
   write('WHAT IS ITS LENGTH IN CM? -->');
   readln(length);
   writeln;
   writeln;
   writeln;
   volume := length*pi*sqr(radius)/2.0;
   writeln('THE VOLUME OF THE CONE IS ',
           volume,' CU. CM.')
END;


PROCEDURE pyramid;

VAR
   height,width,length,volume : real;
```

```
BEGIN
   page(output);
   writeln;
   writeln('CALCULATING THE VOLUME OF A PYRAMID');
   writeln('=========== === ====== == = =======');
   writeln;
   writeln;
   writeln;
   write('WHAT IS ITS HEIGHT IN CM? -->');
   readln(height);
   write('WHAT IS ITS WIDTH IN CM?  -->');
   readln(width);
   write('WHAT IS ITS LENGTH IN CM? -->');
   readln(length);
   writeln;
   writeln;
   writeln;
   volume := height*width*length/2.0;
   writeln('THE VOLUME OF THE PYRAMID IS ',
           volume,' CU. CM.')
END;


PROCEDURE sphere;

CONST
   pi = 3.1416;

VAR
   radius,volume : real;

BEGIN
   page(output);
   writeln;
   writeln('CALCULATING THE VOLUME OF A SPHERE');
   writeln('=========== === ====== == = ======');
   writeln;
   writeln;
   writeln;
   write('WHAT IS ITS RADIUS IN CM? -->');
   readln(radius);
   writeln;
   writeln;
```

```
      writeln;
      volume := (4.0/3.0)*pi*sqr(radius)*radius;
      writeln('THE VOLUME OF THE SPHERE IS ',
              volume,' CU. CM.')
   END;


   BEGIN
      page(output);
      writeln;
      writeln('VOLUMES CALCULATION PROGRAM');
      writeln('======= =========== =======');
      writeln;
      writeln;
      writeln('THE VOLUMES THAT CAN BE CALCULATED ARE :-');
      writeln('     B(OX');
      writeln('     C(YLINDER');
      writeln('     K(ONE');
      writeln('     P(YRAMID');
      writeln('     S(PHERE');
      writeln;
      write('SELECT ONE -->');
      read(ch);
      CASE ch OF
         'B' : box;
         'C' : cylinder;
         'K' : kone;
         'P' : pyramid;
         'S' : sphere
      END
   END.
```

Program 7.3 The volumes calculation program

Program 7.3 calculates the volumes of various geometric solids. Each solid requires different dimensions to be entered into the microcomputer, and must, therefore be handled by a different procedure, which is called as soon as the user selects the volume of the solid he wishes to calculate from the displayed menu. All the variables required for each calculation are declared within that procedure, so that they are available when needed, and not elsewhere, where they will only cause confusion.

7.3 PASSING INFORMATION TO A PROCEDURE

Although it is very useful to split a program up into a series of separate chunks, these chunks would be made much more adaptable, and therefore of use in a far wider range of applications, if information could be transferred to them from the main program, whenever they were called. Take the procedure 'spaces', for example. It would be very useful to be able to call one procedure to write three blank lines, particularly if it were to be done quite often. But what would happen if only two blank lines were wanted, or four, or even five? Slightly different procedures could be written for each of these requirements, but that would hardly be an improvement over the previous situation. If the required number of lines was only to be output once, it would hardly be worth going to the trouble of writing a special procedure, rather than writing the code within the main program itself. If, however the procedure could be told how many blank lines were wanted, only one procedure would need to be written, and the necessary information told to it each time it was called. It is therefore necessary to define some area of global storage that is common to both the main program and the procedure, in which the number of blank lines required can be stored. Since all the variables in the main program are available to the procedure, this can be done by defining a new integer variable, called 'numberoflines', and making sure that it is set to the desired value, before the procedure is called. Program 7.4 shows how this can be done.

```
PROGRAM procexample(input,output);

VAR
   numberoflines : integer;

PROCEDURE spaces;

VAR
   i : integer;

BEGIN
```

```
      FOR i:=1 TO numberoflines DO
         writeln;
   END;

   BEGIN
      page(output);
      numberoflines :=5;
      spaces;
      writeln('THIS IS ANOTHER EXAMPLE OF THE USE OF A PROCEDURE');
      numberoflines := 2;
      spaces;
      writeln('IN THIS CASE, THE NUMBER OF LINES PRINTED,');
      spaces;
      writeln('CAN BE VARIED BY PASSING FURTHER INFORMATION');
      spaces;
      writeln('TO THE PROCEDURE')
   END.
```

Program 7.4 Passing information to a procedure, using global variables

This is a very clumsy way of passing information, although, as shall be seen later, it can sometimes be very useful. It would be much better if the information to be passed could be included within the procedure call. It would then be unnecessary to copy this information into a special variable first. PASCAL provides an extremely useful way of doing this, in the form of the procedure 'parameters'.

The parameters form part of the procedure heading, and are thus accessible to the rest of the program. They are also different from any local variables that are declared within the procedure itself, and are therefore accessible only from within it. What is passed to the procedure is not a copy of the information to be used within it, but a pointer to where it is stored. Only one copy of the information is therefore kept in memory, saving time and space, and considerably easing the programmer's task of keeping track of what information is currently being passed to the procedure.

The parameters must be given names, by which they will be referred to within the procedure, together with the data type of the information that will be transferred through them. In this way the PASCAL compiler ensures that the strict type checking rules are obeyed. The parameters are defined in brackets, following the procedure name, together with their data types, separated by a colon.

The heading for the procedure 'spaces' would therefore look like this:

```
PROCEDURE spaces (numberoflines : integer);
```

and it would be used in the main program by providing the number of blank lines to be printed (this time within brackets) following the procedure name. The following would print four blank lines:

```
  .
  .
spaces(4);
  .
  .
```

Program 7.5 shows how this procedure is used within a program.

```
PROGRAM anotherproc(input,output);

PROCEDURE spaces(numberoflines:integer);

VAR
   i : integer;

BEGIN
   FOR i:=1 TO numberoflines DO
      writeln;
END;

BEGIN
   page(output);
   spaces(5);
   writeln('THIS IS ANOTHER EXAMPLE OF THE USE OF A PROCEDURE');
   spaces(2);
   writeln('IN THIS CASE, THE NUMBER OF LINES PRINTED.');
   spaces(2);
   writeln('CAN BE VARIED BY USING DIFFERENT PARAMETERS');
   spaces(2);
   writeln('WITHIN THE PROCEDURE')
END.
```

Program 7.5 Using a procedure that requires a parameter

7.4 GETTING INFORMATION BACK FROM A PROCEDURE

It is often the case that some results must be returned from a procedure. In PASCAL, there is a clear differentiation between parameters that can and cannot be changed within the procedure. The programmer, therefore, has to decide exactly how each parameter is to be accessed when he writes the procedure heading. Important information can thus be protected from accidental overwriting. It should be noted also, that this form of protection is not available when variables are declared globally, and accessed from within the procedure.. The use of variables that are declared at a higher level should be avoided unless it is absolutely necessary.

To show that the contents of a parameter can be changed within a procedure, its declaration must be preceded by the keyword VAR. For instance, the heading for a procedure that swaps the contents of two real variables, would be:

```
PROCEDURE swap ( VAR x,y : real );
```

where the contents of both x and y are to be changed. The whole procedure is given in program 7.6.

```
PROCEDURE swap(VAR x,y : real);

VAR
   temp : real;

BEGIN
   temp := x;
   x := y;
   y := temp
END;
```

<u>Program</u> <u>7.6</u> A procedure to swap the contents of two parameters

7.5 WRITING YOUR OWN FUNCTIONS

Several special functions have already been met that are available as part of the PASCAL language. These are, in general, the major mathematical functions, such as sin(x), cos(x), ln(x), etc., and various routines to convert data from one data type to another. It is necessary to restrict the number of these routines because they must be available for use in any program. Only those routines that are likely to be of use to the majority of programs can therefore be provided in this way.

PASCAL does, however, provide the means to write one's own functions, in the same way as it does with procedures. The essential difference between a function and a procedure is that a function always returns a value to the calling program, and is therefore used as part of an arithmetic expression. If, for instance, a function 'max' is defined which will return the value of the largest of two parameters, the heading would be:

```
FUNCTION max ( a,b : real ) : real;
```

Once the work of the function has been done, it is necessary to define exactly what value the function is to take, before execution of the main program can be resumed. This is done by assigning the required value to the function in the following way:

```
    .
    .
max := <required value>
    .
    .
```

In general, the layout of a function declaration is:

```
FUNCTION <function name> (<function parameters>)
                          : <function type>;

CONST
     <constant declarations>

VAR
     <variable declarations>

     <further procedure and function declarations>

BEGIN
     <the statements that make up the function>
     <function name> := <expression>
END;
```

The full text of function 'max' is given in program 7.7

```
FUNCTION max(a,b:real):real;

BEGIN
   IF a>=b THEN
      max := a
   ELSE
      max := b
END;
```

Program 7.7 A function to return the larger of two parameters

Except with the simplest procedures, it is necessary to consider what will happen if the data passed to it is inconsistent, or incomplete. For example, when program 7.8 is given the lengths of

```
PROGRAM triangle(input,output);

VAR
   side1,side2,side3 : real;
   angle1,angle2,angle3 : real;
   answer : char;
   finished : boolean;

PROCEDURE angles(x,y,z:real;VAR a,b,c:real);

VAR
   factor : real;
   cosa : real;


FUNCTION asin(x:real) : real;

BEGIN
   asin := atan(x/sqrt(1.0-sqr(x)))
END;
```

```
FUNCTION acos(x:real) : real;

BEGIN
   acos := atan(sqrt(1.0-sqr(x))/x)
END;

BEGIN
   factor := 45.0/atan(1);
   cosa := (y*y+z*z-x*x)/(2*y*z);
   IF abs(cosa)<=1.0 THEN
      BEGIN
         a := acos(cosa)*factor;
         b := asin(y*sqrt(1.0-cosa*cosa)/x)*factor;
         c := 180.0-a-b
      END
   ELSE
      BEGIN
         writeln;
         writeln('ERROR IN ANGLES - NO TRIANGLE POSSIBLE');
         writeln;
         a:=0;
         b:=0;
         c:=0
      END;
END;

BEGIN
   finished := false;
   REPEAT
      page(output);
      writeln;
      writeln('TRIANGLES SOLUTION PROGRAM');
      writeln('========= ======== =======');
      writeln;
      writeln;
      writeln;
      writeln('ENTER THE LENGTHS OF EACH SIDE');
      write('SIDE 1 -->');
      readln(side1);
      write('SIDE 2 -->');
      readln(side2);
      write('SIDE 3 -->');
      readln(side3);
      angles(side1,side2,side3,angle1,angle2,angle3);
```

```
          IF NOT ((abs(angle1)<0.00001) AND
                  (abs(angle2)<0.00001) AND
                  (abs(angle3)<0.00001)) THEN
             BEGIN
                writeln;
                writeln;
                writeln('ANGLE A IS ',angle1);
                writeln('ANGLE B IS ',angle2);
                writeln('ANGLE C IS ',angle3)
             END;
          writeln;
          write('DO YOU WISH TO CALCULATE ANOTHER TRIANGLE? -->');
          read(answer);
          IF answer<>'Y' THEN
             finished := true
       UNTIL finished;
       page(output)
    END.
```

Program 7.8 The triangles solution program

the sides of a triangle: sidex, sidey and sidez, it returns the angles: anglea, angleb and anglec (see figure 7.1). Not all the

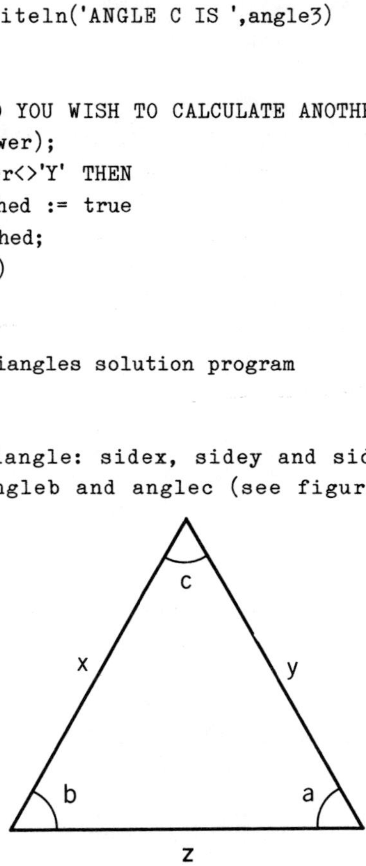

Figure 7.1 The sides and angles of a triangle, as labelled in program 7.8

possible values of sidex, sidey and sidez will be valid, because they may not form a triangle. The procedure must test for this to avoid the possibility of failing with an error message which is meaningless to the user. As it happens, there is a perfectly adequate test to ensure that the sides given make up a triangle, in that

$$\cos(a) = \frac{y^2 + z^2 - x^2}{2xy}$$

from the cosine rule, and for a triangle to exist with the sides given, the following condition must be met:

$$\cos(a) <= 1.0$$

After calculating cos(a), the procedure tests whether a triangle can be formed. If it can, all the angles are calculated. Functions for arcsin(a) and arccos(a) are not provided as part of the PASCAL language, but can be simply constructed from the arctangent function, which is. Each angle is multiplied by a factor to convert it from radians to degrees. If no triangle is possible, the procedure prints out a message to inform the user, and sets all the angles to zero. Since this is an impossible solution, the calling program can test for this result, and take such exception action as is necessary.

7.6 PROBLEMS

7.1 Write a procedure, 'separate', which prints ten spaces on the principal output device, when called.

7.2 Write a procedure:

```
separate(number:integer);
```

which, when called, will print the number of spaces given to it as the parameter number on the principal output device.

7.3 Write a program which will calculate the area of a circle, a triangle, a square, or a ring, depending on which option is selected from a menu by the user.

7.4 A logarithm is defined by the formula:

```
base ^ logarithm = number.
```

Taking the logarithm of both sides, the result is:

log(base ^ logarithm) = log(number)

But this is equivalent to:

logarithm * log(base) = log(number).

Dividing both sides by log(base) the formula for calculating logarithms to any base results:

$$\text{logarithm} = \frac{\text{log(number)}}{\text{log(base)}}.$$

Use this formula to write a function which, when passed a number and a base as parameters, returns its logarithm to that base.

7.5 Write a function which, when passed as parameters a and b, returns the value

$$a^b.$$

7.6 Write a function to return the value of sec(x), where sec(x) is defined as the reciprocal of cos(x).

7.7 Given the laws of Newtonian physics, i.e.

$$v = u + at$$
$$d = s + (u + at)t$$
and $$v^2 = u^2 + 2a(d-s)$$

where
a = acceleration
t = time
d = new distance
s = old distance
v = new velocity
u = old velocity

Define functions giving

(a) the distance covered, given time, original velocity, and acceleration.
(b) the new velocity, given the original velocity, the original distance, the acceleration and the time.

CHAPTER 8

Making Up Tables - The Use of Arrays

8.1 COLLECTING ITEMS OF RELATED DATA TOGETHER

So far, the storage and manipulation of single items of data has been considered. While this is more than sufficient to solve many problems, there are a lot more problems that require whole collections of related information. If, for instance, it is required to count the number of students who have marks in between 0% and 9%, 10% and 19%, etc., and work out what percentage of the total class were in each marks' range, a whole series of different counts would have to be maintained. These could be stored in independent variables, with a different identifier name for each one, but it would be much more convenient if only one name was used, and each individual count could be accessed with the aid of some form of suffix, or subscript. It would then be unnecessary to duplicate code, since to manipulate each count, only the suffix would be changed.

In PASCAL, this can be done using an array. An array is a number of storage elements, all of the same type, which have been grouped together, and are accessed through one identifier. Each individual element is accessed through a subscript, which is placed in square brackets following the identifier name. Suppose the array that stores the number of students in each marks' range is called 'marks'. It would have to be declared at the start of the program not only to be an array containing elements of a particular data type, but also that it contained a certain number of elements arranged in a particular way. The first element of the array (which might be called element 0) would be accessed as follows:

```
marks [0]
```

A suitable data structure in which to store the number of students in each marks' range would be an integer array of ten elements, numbered from 0 to 9. Students with marks in the range i*10 to i*10+9 would then be added to the total stored in the ith element of the array. Figure 8.1 illustrates how this is achieved within the

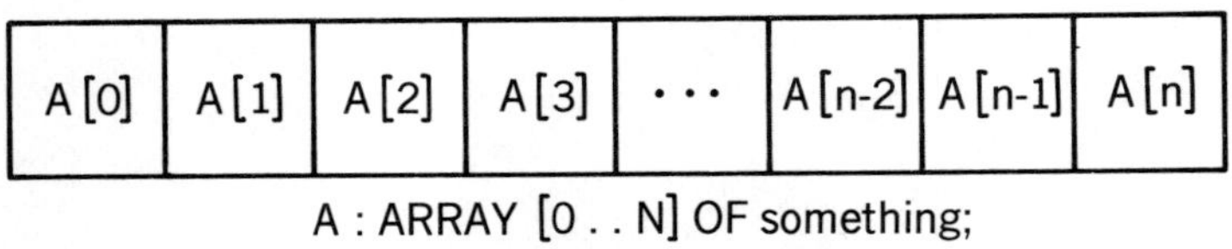

<u>Figure 8.1</u> Storing data items in an array

computer. The subscript does not have to be an integer constant, it can be any variable or expression that yields a value within the declared range of subscripts. This allows each element to be manipulated in turn.

For example, at the start of our marks analysis program, each element will have to be initialised to zero. This can be done using a FOR loop, such as:

```
FOR i := 0 TO 9 DO
   marks [i] := 0;
```

where 'marks' is declared at the start of the program with the following declaration:

```
VAR
   marks : ARRAY [0..9] OF INTEGER;
```

and if a number of different arrays is to be declared a special array type can be declared, and used in any number of variable declarations:

```
TYPE
   markstype = ARRAY [0..9] OF INTEGER;

VAR
   marks : markstype;
```

Now the marks program (program 8.1) will be looked at in some detail. First of all the array 'marks', which is to hold the number of students whose marks are in each category, must be initialised to zero. Then each student's mark is prompted for, and received from the keyboard. Some method of telling the program that it has read

```
PROGRAM marksprog(input,output);

VAR
   marks : ARRAY [0..9] OF integer;
   nostudents : integer;
   allprocessed : boolean;

PROCEDURE clearmarks;

VAR
   i : integer;

BEGIN
   FOR i:=0 TO 9 DO
      marks[i] := 0
END;

PROCEDURE displayheading;

BEGIN
   page(output);
   writeln;
   writeln('STUDENTS'' MARKS ANALYSIS PROGRAM');
   writeln('========= ===== ======== =======');
   writeln;
   writeln;
   writeln;
   writeln('THIS PROGRAM GIVES THE PERCENTAGE OF STUDENTS');
   writeln('OBTAINING MARKS IN EACH GROUP OF TEN MARKS.');
   writeln;
   writeln;
   writeln;
   writeln('ENTER A NEGATIVE MARK TO FINISH');
   writeln;
   writeln
END;
```

```
PROCEDURE readmark;

VAR
   nextmark,markgroup : integer;

BEGIN
   write('NEXT MARK -->');
   readln(nextmark);
   IF nextmark<0 THEN
      allprocessed := true
   ELSE
      BEGIN
         nostudents := nostudents+1;
         markgroup := nextmark DIV 10;
         marks[markgroup] := marks[markgroup]+1
      END
END;

PROCEDURE displayresults;

VAR
   i : integer;
   percent : real;

BEGIN
   page(output);
   writeln;
   writeln('ANALYSIS OF MARKS');
   writeln('======== == =====');
   writeln;
   writeln(nostudents,' MARKS WERE ANALYSED');
   writeln;
   writeln('MARKS GROUP   STUDENTS     % OF TOTAL');
   FOR i:=0 TO 9 DO
   BEGIN
      percent := 100 * marks[i] / nostudents;
      writeln(i*10,'-',i*10+9,' ',marks[i],' ',percent)
   END
END;
```

```
BEGIN
   clearmarks;
   nostudents := 0;
   allprocessed := false;
   displayheading;
   REPEAT
      readmark
   UNTIL allprocessed;
   displayresults
END.
```

Program 8.1 The students' marks program

the last mark must now be devised. This can be done by asking the user to input the total number of students before any other data is requested. The microcomputer can then count the number of marks entered, and will then know when all have been entered. This, however, requires the user to count the number of marks to be entered, a job for which the microcomputer is far better suited. If a special data marker can be identified, the microcomputer can be programmed to keep asking for more data, until this marker is identified. In this case a suitable marker can readily be found, since it is impossible for anyone to get less than zero marks. So if a negative mark is entered, it can be used to signify that all the data has been entered. If there were no suitable data such as this, the microcomputer could be programmed to ask whether there is any more, before prompting for the next mark. If the answer is no, then it knows that it has finished. If the program then displays the number of marks received, this is a useful check to ensure that the expected number of marks have been entered.

As each mark is received, it is assigned to a category, and one is added to that count. A count is also kept of the total number of marks received, so that the total can be checked with the user, and the percentage of students in each range can be calculated. Once all the marks have been analysed, the information is displayed, as required. The final program is given in program 8.1.

8.2 TABLES OF INFORMATION

It is often necessary to pass whole tables of information to a procedure, so that it can perform the required task. This has to be done using arrays. In PASCAL, the number of data items that can be stored in an array is an integral part of the data type definition, and, therefore, an array that contains a different number of elements of the same type, or has different required bounds, is of a different data type. It is only possible to pass parameters to procedures if the variable declaration in the calling program, and the dummy parameter in the procedure, are both of the same data type. Although there are good reasons for this, in that it makes for a smaller and more efficient compiler, it does make the passing of arrays as parameters rather awkward. In the extreme, it could mean that a different procedure must be written for each array that is to be processed.

There is, however, a relatively simple, if inelegant, way of avoiding this problem. If all arrays are declared to be of one type, a type which allows sufficient elements for the largest number of parameters likely to be required, another parameter can then be used to pass the largest subscript that actually contains useful information. While this can waste a considerable amount of memory, since in some arrays all the elements are unlikely ever to be used, it does simplify the programming to a great extent.

To illustrate this, a procedure can be looked at that integrates the area under a curve, using Simpson's rule. The formula for a function f(x), to be integrated over the range from x=a to x=b, divided into n equal intervals, is:

$$\int_a^b f(x)\,dx = (2*interval/3)*(f(a)+f(b)+\sum_{i=1}^{n} (i \bmod 2)*f(a+i*interval))$$

(n must be even)

where the interval is defined as:

$$interval = (a-b)/n$$

(see figure 8.2). It is possible in standard PASCAL (but not in most microcomputer implementations of the language) to pass the function as a parameter. This is useful, so long as it is known when the program is written. In many cases, particularly when experimental results are to be analysed, this is not so, and only the values at regular points along the curve are available. It is then necessary to pass an array containing this information to the integration procedure. If this array is of a standard size, any data up to the maximum number of points allowed by a constant definition at the top of the program can be satisfactorily analysed. Program 8.2

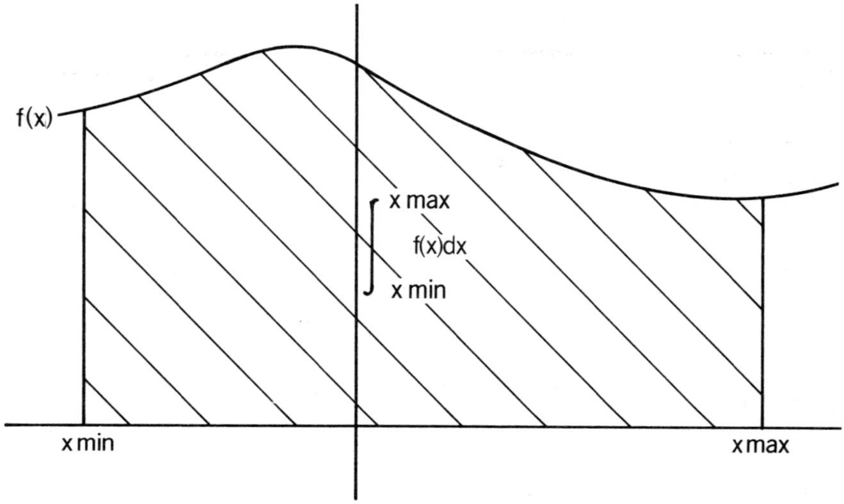

Figure 8.2 Integrating a curve using Simpson's rule

illustrates such a routine, together with a test routine, which fills the function table with the values given by the function:

$$f(x) = x^4 - 3x^3 - 4x^2 + 3x - 6.$$

It should be noted how the function is calculated within the program, as with the aid of a little rearrangement, the total number of arithmetic operations, and hence the speed of execution, has been considerably enhanced. It is often possible to do this, and with the relative slowness of microcomputers when performing arithmetic operations, it can add greatly to the usefulness of the program.

```
PROGRAM simpson (input,output);

CONST
   maxftablelngth = 100;

TYPE
   novalues = 0..maxftablelngth;
   valuetable = ARRAY[0..maxftablelngth] OF real;
```

```
VAR
   functable : valuetable;
   upperbound,lowerbound : real;
   nointervals : novalues;
   xinterval : real;
   x : real;
   integral : real;
   errorflag : boolean;
   i : novalues;

FUNCTION f(x:real):real;

BEGIN
    f := ((((x-3)*x-4)*x+3)*x)-6
END;

FUNCTION integrate(funcvalues:valuetable;
                   n:novalues;
                   interval:real;
                   VAR error:boolean
                   ):real;

VAR
   sum : real;
   i : integer;

BEGIN
   IF odd(n) THEN
      BEGIN
         writeln('THE NUMBER OF VALUES GIVEN MUST BE ODD');
         integrate := 0.0;
         error := true
      END
   ELSE
      BEGIN
         error := false;
         sum := 0.5*(funcvalues[0]+funcvalues[n]);
         FOR i:= 1 TO n-1 DO
            sum := sum+(i MOD 2+1)*funcvalues[i];
         integrate := 2.0*interval*sum/3.0
      END
END;
```

```
BEGIN
   page(output);
   writeln;
   write('A PROGRAM TO TEST A SIMPSON''S RULE');
   writeln(' INTEGRATION FUNCTION.');
   write('= ======= == ==== = ========= ====');
   writeln(' =================== ');
   writeln;
   writeln;
   writeln('THE FUNCTION TO BE INTEGRATED IS :-');
   writeln;
   writeln('        X^4-3*X^3-4*X^2+3*X-6');
   writeln;
   writeln;
   writeln('PLEASE SUPPLY THE LOWER AND UPPER BOUNDS OF THE');
   writeln('INTEGRATION, AND THE NUMBER OF INTERVALS THAT ARE');
   writeln('TO BE USED, (MUST BE LESS THAN ',
           maxftablelngth,')');
   writeln;
   write('ENTER THE LOWER BOUND OF X -->');
   readln(lowerbound);
   write('ENTER THE UPPER BOUND OF X -->');
   readln(upperbound);
   REPEAT
      write('NO. OF INTERVALS TO BE USED (MUST BE EVEN) -->');
      readln(nointervals)
   UNTIL(NOT odd(nointervals))
             AND (nointervals<=maxftablelngth);
   xinterval :=(upperbound-lowerbound)/nointervals;
   FOR i:=0 TO nointervals DO
   BEGIN
      x := lowerbound+i*xinterval;
      functable[i] := f(x)
   END;
   integral := integrate
                (functable,nointervals,xinterval,errorflag);
   IF errorflag THEN
      BEGIN
         write('AN EVEN NUMBER OF INTERVALS ');
         writeln('(OR A ODD NUMBER OF VALUES)');
         write('MUST BE GIVEN FOR A SIMPSON''S ');
         writeln('RULE INTEGRATION')
      END
   ELSE
```

```
        BEGIN
           writeln;
           writeln;
           writeln('THE VALUE OF THE INTEGRAL IS',integral)
        END
    END.
```

Program 8.2 The Simpson's rule integration program

8.3 MATRICES

PASCAL allows arrays to be declared with more than one dimension. This allows programs to be written, which manipulate matrices. The problem of needing to declare the subscript range as part of the data type is still present. As in the last section, a standard type definition can be used, and parameters passed to the procedure for each dimension, to give the largest subscript used.

A suitable definition would be:

```
    CONST
       maxsize = 10;

    TYPE
       matrix = ARRAY [0..maxsize,0..maxsize] OF real;
```

By declaring maxsize as a constant, it is a simple matter to change the amount of storage allocated. Should this need changing for any reason, only one line of code will have to be altered, and that is at the top of the program, where it is very easy to find. This constant should also be used anywhere in the program, where the top size of the matrix is needed, rather than the equivalent integer constant. This avoids many of the niggling editing errors that tend to occur whenever a program must be changed in many places.

```
    TYPE
        matrix = ARRAY [0..maxsize,0..maxsize] OF real;


    PROCEDURE matadd (mat1,mat2 : matrix; horder,vorder : integer;
                      VAR matsum : matrix);
```

```
VAR i,j : 0..maxsize;

BEGIN
   FOR j:=0 TO vorder DO
      FOR i:=0 TO horder DO
         matsum[i,j] := mat1[i,j] + mat2[i,j]
END;
```

Program 8.3 A matrix addition routine

Program 8.3 is a matrix addition routine that shows how this works. Mat1 and mat2 are the matrices to be added, both being of the type matrix, just defined. The required elements are from 0 to horder, and from 0 to vorder. Matsum is another parameter, of type matrix, in which the result is to be returned. Since, by the rules of matrix arithmetic, all the matrices must be the same size, this is all the information that is required. The addition is performed one element at a time, within the two loops.

Matrix multiplication is somewhat more complicated, as each element is made up from the sum of the elements in the original matrices. Thus each element of a product matrix C is formed from the elements of matrices A and B, in the following way:

$$C(i,j) = \sum_{i=1}^{n} A(i,k)B(k,j)$$

where n is the horizontal order of matrix A. Program 8.4 shows how this is implemented in PASCAL.

```
TYPE
    matrix = ARRAY [0..maxsize,0..maxsize] OF real;


PROCEDURE matmult (mat1,mat2 : matrix; horder,vorder : integer;
                  VAR matproduct : matrix);

VAR i,j,k : 0..maxsize;

BEGIN
   FOR j:=0 TO vorder DO
      FOR i:=0 TO horder DO
```

```
          BEGIN
             temp := 0.0;
             FOR k:=0 TO horder DO
                temp := mat1[i,k]*mat2[k,j];
             matproduct[i,j] := temp
          END
     END;
```

Program 8.4 A matrix multiplication routine

8.4 PACKED ARRAYS

It is usual on most computer systems to store the elements of an array one to each basic storage element or word of memory. In this way, it is possible to ensure that each individual item can be accessed as efficiently as possible, thus saving valuable execution time. This is fine so long as each item stored requires one, or more, complete memory bytes. If, however, the data can be stored in much less than one complete word, then the rest of the word cannot be used. This is not too serious when the program is to be run on a large mainframe computer, where there is usually more than sufficient memory available, but when it is to be run on a microcomputer, with very limited storage capacity, this can be very restricting. In particular, a lot of memory can be saved if arrays of boolean, or character variables, can be stored in a much more densely-packed form, as only a small fraction of each word would be used.

PASCAL allows the programmer to specify that all the elements of an array are to be packed as tightly as possible, by placing as many elements as there is space available for in each word. Figure 8.3 illustrates how this is achieved. In this way, the programmer has the choice of either maximising the amount of useful information that can be stored in the available memory (at the expense of somewhat slower access to that information) or arranging the information in such a way that it can be accessed as rapidly as possible, but with some waste of storage capacity.

It is necessary to indicate in the array declaration that it is to be stored in packed form, by including the keyword PACKED before ARRAY. So that, for instance, if an array of ten boolean flags is to be declared and stored in packed form, the programmer would write

```
flags : PACKED ARRAY [0..9] OF boolean;
```

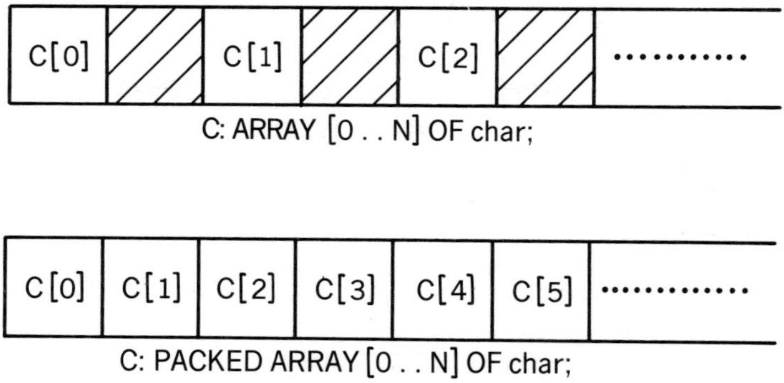

Figure 8.3 The difference between packed and ordinary arrays

It is sometimes necessary to transfer the contents of a packed array to an unpacked array, or vice versa. PASCAL provides two standard procedures 'pack' and 'unpack' to allow this. Thus, if two arrays are declared as follows:

```
VAR
   a : ARRAY [m..n] OF something;
   b : PACKED ARRAY [p..q] OF something;
```

where something has been previously defined as a suitable data type, the operation of pack and unpack is as follows:

pack (a,base,b)	copies each element of a into the corresponding element of b, starting from base, which is copied into the first element of b.
unpack (b,a,base)	copies each element of b into the corresponding element of a, starting with the first element of b, which is copied to base in a.

8.5 STRINGS

One very useful application of arrays is the storage and manipulation of series of characters, in the form of strings. A string consists of two, or more, characters in a particular order. They allow words, phrases, and even complete sentences to be held within the microcomputer's memory, so that they can be analysed, used to give more meaningful output, or simply stored for future reference.

As has already been seen, in PASCAL it is necessary to define the number of elements required in an array, when it is declared. With strings, this is virtually impossible, since it is not known how many characters will be needed to store all the words, or how many phrases need be stored. Take, for instance, a program to record all the marks obtained by the students in a class. It is necessary to print out a list of all the students' names, followed by the marks they obtained in individual examinations, their total score, and the percentage of full marks obtained. Unfortunately the exact number of characters in the longest student's name is not known when the program is being written. It is therefore necessary to make a reasonable guess as to the number which may be expected, and to ensure that enough storage is declared for the longest likely eventuality.

Some of the PASCAL compilers available for use on microcomputers (notably the UCSD implementation) have solved this problem in another way. A special data type, STRING, has been added to the basic types defined as part of the PASCAL language. This data structure has a size sufficient to hold all the characters in the string to be stored, and the housekeeping necessary is dealt with at a lower level, within the compiler and run-time sub-routine package that is supplied with it. Various manipulative functions, such as concatonation, finding occurrences of particular character sequences, etc., are dealt with by the provision of special additional procedures. This has the particular advantage that it is no longer necessary to guess how long a string is likely to be, and therefore memory is less likely to be wasted. It does mean, however, that programs are no longer written in standard PASCAL, and cannot, therefore, be run on another system, unless the particular compiler with which the program was developed is also available on that system.

The method of handling strings described here is, however, compatible with standard PASCAL, and will therefore work with any compiler that adequately supports the accepted standard. A string can best be manipulated as a packed array of characters, for which a special data type, called ALPHA, can be defined to avoid confusion with the special data type available with some compilers. A suitable declaration would therefore be:

```
alpha : PACKED ARRAY [0..maxalphlength] OF CHAR;
```

where 'maxalphlength' is given a suitable value by a constant definition. In this way, if it is found desirable to change the maximum number of characters that are stored in the strings at a later stage, this can be done by simply editing one line, and recompiling.

It is now necessary to consider how the characters are to be stored in the array. The simplest method is to store them from element 0 up, in the order that they are found, and filling the rest of the character positions with spaces. Figure 8.4 illustrates this. The

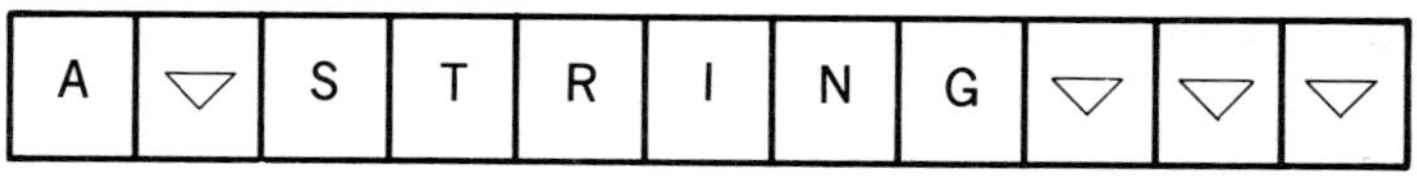

(▽ =space character)

Figure 8.4 The storage of strings

disadvantage is that an empty string (i.e. one that contains no characters) is not differentiated from one that contains only spaces. In most applications this is not a great disadvantage, and can be overcome by defining some suitable special character to be the end-of-string marker, and ensuring that it is always stored as the last character (see figure 8.4). For the purposes of illustration, the first alternative will be used in the examples discussed here.

It is now necessary to look at how routines can be written to manipulate the contents of strings; firstly how a string can be read into the computer, and printed out when needed. Program 8.5 shows this, together with a simple routine to see how many characters it

```
PROGRAM stringread(input,output);

CONST
   maxalpha = 80;

TYPE
   alpha = PACKED ARRAY [1..maxalpha] OF char;
```

```
VAR
   str : alpha;

FUNCTION length(a:alpha) : integer;

VAR
   tlength : 1..maxalpha;

BEGIN
   tlength := maxalpha;
   WHILE a[tlength]=' ' DO
      tlength := tlength-1;
      length:=tlength
END;

PROCEDURE aread(VAR a:alpha);

VAR
   i : 1..maxalpha;
   ch: char;

BEGIN
   i := 1;
   REPEAT
      read(ch);
      a[i] := ch;
      i := i+1
   UNTIL eoln(input);
   WHILE i<maxalpha DO
   BEGIN
      a[i] := ' ';
      i := i+1
   END;
   a[i] := ' '
END;

BEGIN
   page(output);
   writeln;
   writeln('A SIMPLE STRING READING PROGRAM.');
   writeln('= ====== ====== ======= =======');
```

```
   writeln;
   writeln;
   write('ENTER A STRING -->');
   aread(str);
   writeln('IT CONTAINED ',length(str),' CHARACTERS.')
END.
```

Program 8.5 Reading and writing strings

contains. Using 'aread', the entry of a string is terminated by pressing the return key. This is a clear and unambiguous sign, which soon becomes automatic with the user. Indeed most of the programs in this book are written to accept single character commands directly, but to wait until return is pressed before accepting the entry.

```
PROGRAM colourcodes(input,output);

CONST
   maxalpha = 10;
   blank    = '          ';

TYPE
   alpha = PACKED ARRAY [1..maxalpha] OF char;

VAR
   bandcolour : ARRAY [0..11] OF alpha;
   done       : boolean;

FUNCTION length(a:alpha) : integer;

VAR
   tlength : 1..maxalpha;
BEGIN
   tlength := maxalpha;
   WHILE a[tlength]=' ' DO
      tlength := tlength-1;
      length:=tlength
END;
```

```
PROCEDURE aread(VAR a:alpha);

VAR
   i : 1..maxalpha;
   ch: char;

BEGIN
   a := blank;
   i := 1;
   REPEAT
      read(ch);
      a[i] := ch;
      i := i+1
   UNTIL eoln(input)
END;

FUNCTION poweroften(power:integer):real;

VAR
   i : integer;
   factor,temp : real;

BEGIN
   IF power=0 THEN
      poweroften := 1
   ELSE
      BEGIN
         IF power<0 THEN
            BEGIN
               factor := 0.1;
               power := -power
            END
         ELSE
            factor := 10.0;
         temp := 1;
         FOR i:=1 TO power DO
             temp := temp*factor;
         poweroften := temp
      END
END;
```

```
PROCEDURE awrite(a:alpha);

VAR
   i : 1..maxalpha;

BEGIN
   FOR i:=1 TO length(a) DO
      write(a[i])
END;

PROCEDURE initialise;

BEGIN
   bandcolour[ 0] := 'BLACK     ';
   bandcolour[ 1] := 'BROWN     ';
   bandcolour[ 2] := 'RED       ';
   bandcolour[ 3] := 'ORANGE    ';
   bandcolour[ 4] := 'YELLOW    ';
   bandcolour[ 5] := 'GREEN     ';
   bandcolour[ 6] := 'BLUE      ';
   bandcolour[ 7] := 'PURPLE    ';
   bandcolour[ 8] := 'GREY      ';
   bandcolour[ 9] := 'WHITE     ';
   bandcolour[10] := 'GOLD      ';
   bandcolour[11] := 'SILVER    '
END;

PROCEDURE interpretcodes(VAR finished:boolean);

VAR
   firstband ,secondband ,thirdband  : integer;
   answer : char;

PROCEDURE displaycolours;

VAR
   i : 0..9;

BEGIN
   FOR i:=0 TO 9 DO
```

```
        BEGIN
           awrite(bandcolour[i]);
           write(', ')
        END;
        writeln
     END;

     FUNCTION bandvalue(colour:alpha):integer;

     VAR
        found : boolean;
        i : integer;

     BEGIN
        i:=0;
        found := false;
        REPEAT
           IF colour=bandcolour[i] THEN
              BEGIN
                 bandvalue:=i;
                 found:=true
              END;
           i:=i+1
        UNTIL (i=12) OR found;
        IF NOT found THEN
           bandvalue:=-1;
     END;

     FUNCTION readcolour : integer;

     VAR
        accepted : boolean;
        thisband : alpha;
        colourvalue : integer;

     BEGIN
        REPEAT
           accepted := true;
           aread(thisband);
           colourvalue := bandvalue(thisband);
```

```
      IF colourvalue=-1 THEN
         BEGIN
            accepted := false;
            write('THIS IS NOT A USUAL COLOUR,',
             ' PLEASE CHECK AND RETYPE -->')
    END
   UNTIL accepted;
   readcolour := colourvalue
END;

PROCEDURE displayvalue(first,second,third:integer);

VAR
   value : real;
   units : alpha;

BEGIN
   IF third=10 THEN
      third := -1
   ELSE
      IF third=11 THEN
         third := -2;
   IF third >= 5 THEN
      BEGIN
         units := 'MEGOHMS   ';
         third := third-6;
      END
   ELSE
      IF third >= 2 THEN
         BEGIN
            units := 'KILOHMS   ';
            third := third-3
         END
      ELSE
         units := 'OHMS      ';
   value := (first*10+second)*poweroften(third);
   write(value,' ');
   awrite(units);
   writeln
END;
```

```
BEGIN
   page(output);
   writeln;
   writeln;
   writeln('A PROGRAM TO INTERPRET RESISTOR COLOUR CODES');
   writeln('= ======= == ========= ======== ====== =====');
   writeln;
   writeln;
   writeln('THIS PROGRAM INTERPRETS THE COLOUR CODED BANDS, ');
   writeln('WHICH GIVE THE RESISTANCE VALUE.');
   writeln;
   writeln('THESE BANDS ARE THE THREE, STARTING WITH THE ONE ');
   writeln('CLOSEST TO ONE END OF THE BODY OF THE RESISTOR');
   writeln;
   writeln('ALLOWABLE COLOURS ARE :-');
   displaycolours;
   writeln;
   write('ENTER THE COLOUR OF THE FIRST BAND -->');
   firstband := readcolour;
   write('ENTER THE COLOUR OF THE SECOND BAND -->');
   secondband := readcolour;
   write('ENTER THE VALUE OF THE THIRD BAND -->');
   thirdband := readcolour;
   writeln;
   writeln;
   write('THE VALUE OF THIS RESISTOR IS ');
   displayvalue(firstband,secondband,thirdband);
   writeln;
   writeln;
   write('DO YOU WISH TO LOOK AT ANOTHER RESISTOR (Y/N) -->');
   read(answer);
   IF answer='Y' THEN
      finished := false
   ELSE
      finished := true
END;
```

```
BEGIN
   initialise;
   done:=false;
   REPEAT
      interpretcodes(done)
   UNTIL done
END.
```

Program 8.6 A program to interpret resistor colour codes

To show how these routines would be used in a program, program 8.6 has been included. This program accepts the colours of the first three bands of a resistor, which signify its value, interprets them, and displays its resistance in ohms. It is a useful tutorial aid for anyone who is not completely familiar with these codes. The method of comparing the strings entered with the table of expected words should be noted. When the table is filled at the start of the program, all the character positions, including those beyond the end of the word, must be specified explicitly, hence the spaces after each word. It is then possible to declare the contents of each string directly, in the function 'bandvalue', to start the decoding process which is completed in 'readcolour', and 'displayvalue'.

Another way in which a string can be used is to store a series of letters, one of which is to be selected for printing, depending on the value of some variable. Program 8.7 is a procedure to print a byte of information (in PASCAL, a byte can be simulated by a subrange of 0 to 255) as two hexadecimal digits. In this routine the string is used as an array and the character is selected by its subscript.

```
TYPE
   byte = 0..255;

PROCEDURE writebyte(abyte:byte);

CONST
   maxhexdigit = 15;

TYPE
   digitstring = PACKED ARRAY[0..maxhexdigit] OF char;
```

```
VAR
   firstdigit,seconddigit : 0..15;
   hexdigits : digitstring;

BEGIN
   hexdigits := '0123456789ABCDEF';
   firstdigit := abyte DIV 16;
   seconddigit := abyte MOD 16;
   write(hexdigits[firstdigit],hexdigits[seconddigit])
END;
```

Program 8.7 A procedure to write out a byte as two hexadecimal digits

Further routines can be written, which allow the contents of strings to be manipulated, including inserting and deleting characters, determining whether a given sub-string is present, and so on. Program 8.8 gives only one example, a procedure to concatonate two strings. This is of interest, as a possible error condition is that there may be too many characters in the combined string to store within the declared data structure. An error message must then be printed, and a suitable recovery made. In this case, since the result would be returned in the first string variable, it is sensible to fill it to the number of characters available.

```
CONST
   maxline=80;

TYPE
   alpha=ARRAY[1..maxline] OF char;

PROCEDURE concat(string1,string2:alpha;
                 VAR destination:alpha);

VAR
   i,length1,length2:1..maxline;

BEGIN
   length1:=length(string1);
   length2:=length(string2);
```

```
        IF (length1+length2)>maxline THEN
           writeln('STRINGS TOO LONG')
        ELSE
           BEGIN
              FOR i:=1 TO length1 DO
                 destination[i]:=string1[i];
              FOR i:=1 TO length2 DO
                 destination[length1+i]:=string2[i]
           END
     END;
```

Program 8.8 A procedure to concatonate two strings. The function 'length' used is that given in program 8.5

8.6 PROBLEMS

8.1 Write a function which takes as a parameter a 2x2 matrix, and returns as its value the determinant.

8.2 Write a function which takes as parameters two strings, and returns zero, if the first string does not contain the second, or, if it does, returns the character position of the first character.

8.3 Write a procedure to delete a sub-string from a character string.

8.4 Write a program, which will read in a number, and display it to base 2, 8, 10 or 16, as selected by the user.

8.5 Write a procedure that takes as parameters an array of numbers, and the number of elements containing useful information into numerical order.

8.6 Another method of integration, apart from Simpson's rule, is the trapezoid rule, in which the area under the curve is approximated by a number of trapeziums, of equal width (see figure 8.5).

The area of the ith trapezium is given by:

$$\frac{[f(i) + f(i+1)]\Delta x}{2}$$

Since the right-hand side of each trapezium is also the left-hand

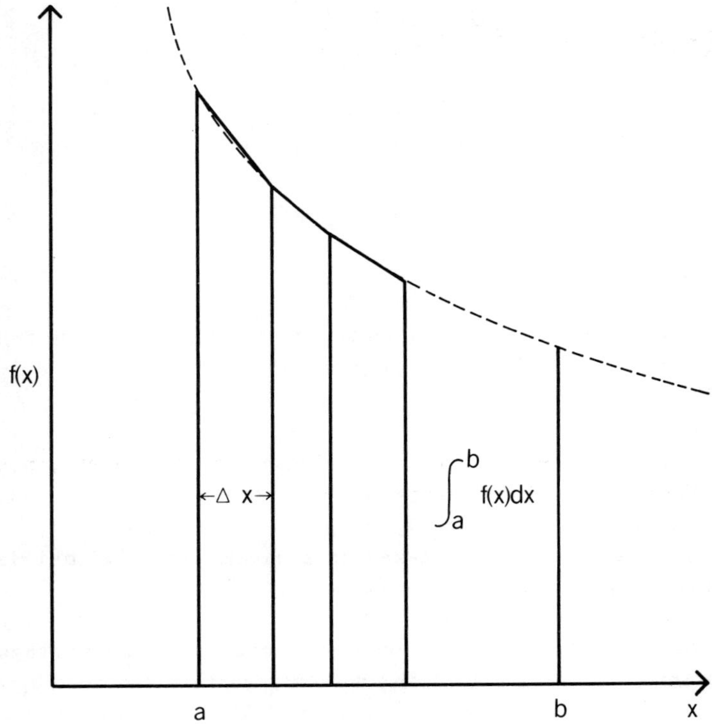

Figure 8.5 The division of the area under a curve into trapeziums

side of the next, the area under the curve is approximated by:

$$\int_a^b f(x)dx = [f(a) + 2f(1) + 2f(2) + \ldots$$
$$2f(n-2) + 2f(n-1) + f(b)]\frac{\Delta x}{2}$$

where n is the number of trapeziums into which the area is divided.

Write a procedure, similar to 'integrate' in program 8.2, which uses the trapezoid rule. Compare the results obtained using this routine with those using the Simpson's rule routine in the original program.

CHAPTER 9
Sets in PASCAL

9.1 THE USE OF SETS

In PASCAL, a set is defined as a collection of data items, all of the same data type. It is possible to construct a set, either by assigning values to it, or by interaction with other sets, and it is possible to test whether a data item of the right type is a member of the set. In addition it is possible to obtain the next or the preceding item of the set. The data type of the objects which belong to the set is usually called the base type of the set. This may be any scalar type, but not a structured data type. For example:

```
TYPE
   language = (english,french,german,russian,spanish,italian);

VAR
   setoflanguage = SET OF language;
```

or:

```
TYPE
   character = 'a'..'z';

VAR
   setofchar : SET OF character;
```

Usually the number of data items that are members of a set is comparatively small, so most compiler writers place some limit on the number of items that can be included in a set. This is typically in the range of 64 to 256 data items, which is more than sufficient for almost all normal purposes.

The simplest way of constructing a set is to list its elements.

This is done within square brackets, to signify that they are members of the set. Thus the following are all appropriate assignments to the 'setofchar' defined above.

```
    setofchar := ['a','b','c','d'];
    setofchar := ['a','e','i','o','u'];
    setofchar := ['c','d','f','t','z'];
    setofchar := ['a'..'z']
or
    setofchar := ['i'..'n'];
```

It should be noted that the symbol (..) can be used to specify that the two values listed, and every value between them are to be included within the set. ['a'..'z'] thus includes all the letters within the set. It is also possible for the set to have no members at all, which would be written:

```
    setofchar := [];
```

and would be known as an empty set.

In addition, there are three operators that have special meanings when applied to sets. These are:

```
    +        union
    *        intersection
and -        difference.
```

The union of two sets is a new set that contains all the elements of the other two. Thus, if two sets are defined, one of which contains all the alphabet, and the other, all the decimal digits:

```
TYPE
   setofchar = SET OF char;

VAR
   letters,digits,lettersanddigits : setofchar;

BEGIN
   letters := ['a'..'z'];
   digits  := ['0'..'9'];
   lettersanddigits := letters+digits;
```

'Lettersanddigits' would then contain all the letters and all the digits (see figure 9.1).

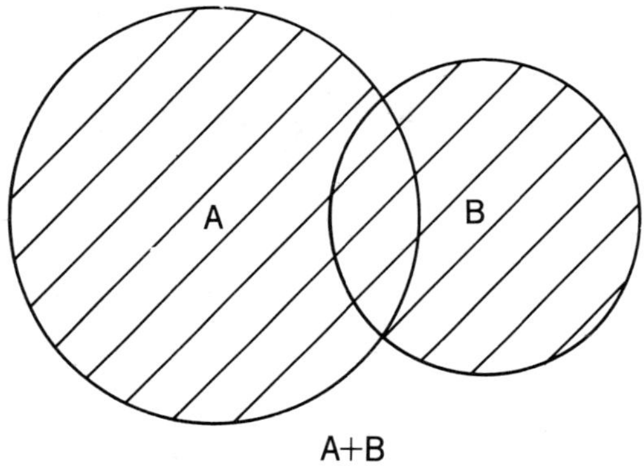

Figure 9.1 The union of two sets

Similarly the intersection of two sets is a new set that contains all the elements that are common to both. Thus, if one set is defined to contain the first half of the alphabet, and another to contain just the vowels:

```
letters := ['a'..'m']
vowels :=  ['a','e','i','o','u'];
letters := letters*vowels;
```

letters would now contain just 'a', 'e' and 'i' (see figure 9.2).

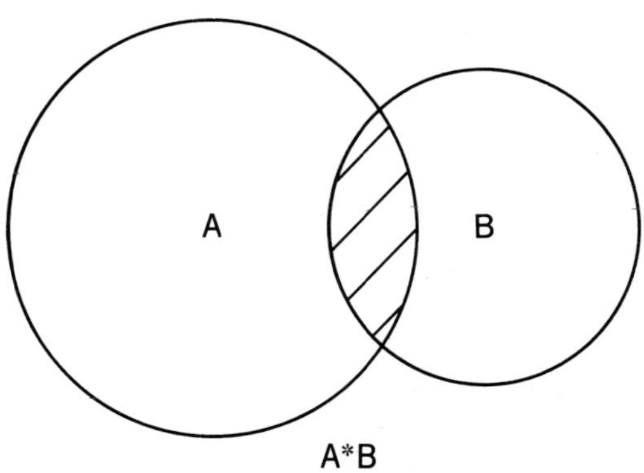

Figure 9.2 The intersection of two sets

Finally the difference operator allows us to pick out those elements that are not members of either set (see figure 9.3). For

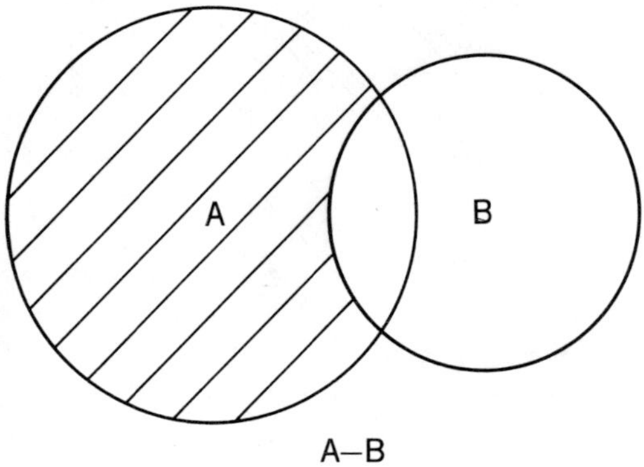

Figure 9.3 The difference between two sets

instance, if only the consonants are to be considered, rather than writing them all out explicitly, which would make for rather a complicated expression, the programmer might write:

```
letters := ['a'..'z'];
vowels :=  ['a','e','i','o','u'];
consonants := letters-vowels;
```

With these operations it is possible to construct sets to serve many purposes in PASCAL. As shall be seen in the rest of this chapter, one of the most important uses is to test character input, so as to protect the user of a program from difficulties that might result from pressing the wrong key when he is asked for some input.

9.2 THE USE OF RELATIONAL OPERATORS WITH SETS

In addition to the operators that act on two sets, there are relational operators that compare their contents. These are:

```
     =      denotes set equality.
     <>     denotes set inequality.
     <=     denotes 'is contained in'.
and  >=     denotes 'contains'.
```

where equality means that both sets contain exactly the same members.

Inequality is therefore when the two sets do not contain the same members. A set is included in another set if all its elements are also members of that set, and equally, if a set contains another set, all the elements of that set are contained within it. These last two operators can be used to test whether a set is a sub-set of another.

9.3 TESTING FOR INCLUSION WITHIN SETS

There is one other operator that is used only in conjunction with sets. That is the test as to whether an expression is a member of a set, and this is denoted by the PASCAL keyword, IN. This operator takes an expression that yields a value of the base type, and gives a value of TRUE, if it is a member of the set, and FALSE otherwise. So the general syntax is:

```
     <expression> IN <set>
```

and typical examples of its use would include:

```
     'a' IN vowels;
     ch IN letters;
and  ch IN ['y','n'];
```

This is a very powerful facility, which can be used to great effect. Take, for instance, program 9.1. This is a function which takes as its argument a character, and returns that character unless it is an upper case letter, in which case it returns the lower case equivalent. The IN operator is used to select out just those characters that are to be changed, all the others being simply copied over. To make the change, a knowledge of the values of the ASCII character codes used by most microcomputers to represent the characters within the computer's memory (see Appendix A) is used. Since all the character codes follow each other in the order of the alphabet, it is only necessary to convert the character to its integer code equivalent, using the built-in 'ord' function, add the difference between the codes for the lower-case character codes to it, and convert back to a character using the 'chr' function.

```
FUNCTION convert(ch:char):char;

VAR
   i:integer;

BEGIN
   IF ch IN ['A'..'Z'] THEN
      BEGIN
         i:=ord(ch);
         i:=i+32;
         convert:=chr(i)
      END
   ELSE
      convert:=ch
END;
```

Program 9.1 A function that converts upper case characters into lower case

9.4 THE USE OF SETS - TESTING FOR APPROPRIATE INPUT

Another use of sets is to determine whether characters input from the keyboard are acceptable, or not. So far when asking for a yes or no answer, all the programs that have been looked at have tested for one alternative, and assumed the other, if the right character was not found. This is far from satisfactory, as the user might have pressed a wrong key by mistake, and then he has no way of recovering from his mistake. Program 9.2 is a function that returns TRUE, if the user says yes, and FALSE if he says no, but keeps repeating the question until a meaningful answer is received. This protects the user from himself, in a way that is most important when a program is to be used by others who are not familiar with its operation, and may well have little knowledge of how a computer works, and what is likely to be acceptable as an answer to this type of question.

```
FUNCTION yesorno : boolean;

VAR
   ch : char;

BEGIN
   REPEAT
      read(ch);
      writeln
   UNTIL ch IN ['Y','y','N','n'];
   yesorno := ch IN ['Y','y']
END;
```

Program 9.2 The 'yesorno' function

Program 9.3 is a similar function that is designed to accept a hexadecimal number typed in from the keyboard, and to return its value as an integer quantity. It is important that only those characters that represent hexadecimal digits are accepted, anything else must be an error, except for 'return', which terminates the number. Again a set is defined to contain those characters that are to be accepted, any other character causes processing to cease, the prompt to reappear, and the user has to start again.

```
FUNCTION readhex : integer;

VAR
   ch : char;
   num : integer;
   total : integer;
   digits,letters : SET OF char;

BEGIN
   total := 0;
   digits := ['0'..'9'];
   letters := ['A'..'F'];
   read(ch);
```

```
        WHILE (ch IN digits) OR (ch IN letters) DO
           BEGIN
              IF ch IN digits THEN
                 num := ord(ch)-ord('0')
              ELSE
                 num := (ord(ch)-ord('A'))+10;
              total := total*16+num;
              read(ch)
           END;
        readhex := total
     END;
```

Program 9.3 A function to read a hexadecimal number, and return its decimal equivalent

9.5 MENU-DRIVEN PROGRAMS

A number of programs have already used single-character input to select one of a series of options with the help of a CASE statement. This is fine, so long as the character input is one of those for which there is a branch in the CASE statement. If there is not, an execution error would result in standard PASCAL, or for those compilers that attempt to recover from this problem, different action would result when using different compilers, depending on what error recovery the compiler attempts.

It would be possible to test for each of the allowable commands with a series of conditions, using IF statements. This would rapidly become totally unwieldy if there were more than two or three options. However, if a set is constructed containing all the acceptable options, it is then possible to test the input to see whether it is allowable before entering the CASE statement. If it is not acceptable, the prompt line can then be redisplayed, and the user can try again. This is a much better user interface than the user being given an undecipherable (to him) error message, and having to start the program run from scratch, when, possibly, a lot of data had been entered.

It may be useful, for instance, to write a program that converts angles given in degrees to radians, and vice versa. A one-character command can be used to select which way the conversion is to be performed. A CASE statement can then be used to select the option chosen. The obvious choices for the single-letter commands are 'd' and 'r', which could be checked using a condition. It would be a better user interface, however, if the program could accept both the upper-case and lower-case characters as valid commands, as this would save the naive user from confusion when he types a command in the wrong case. To handle this with conditions would now lead to considerable complexity, whereas testing that the command is valid, using a set of those acceptable, and CASE statements to select which of the conversions is required, leads to a much more elegant program, as program 9.4 shows.

```
PROGRAM conversion2(input,output);

CONST
    pi=3.14159;

VAR
    ch:char;
    angle:real;

FUNCTION yesorno : boolean;

VAR
   ch : char;

BEGIN
   REPEAT
      write('[Y(ES OR N(O]');
      read(ch);
      writeln
   UNTIL ch IN ['Y','N','y','n'];
   yesorno := ch IN ['Y','y']
END;

BEGIN
    REPEAT
       page(output);
       writeln;
       writeln;
       writeln('A PROGRAM TO CONVERT ANGLES');
       writeln('= ======= == ======= ======');
       writeln;
```

```
            writeln;
            writeln('CONVERT TO RADIANS (R)');
            writeln;
            writeln('     OR TO DEGREES (D)');
            writeln;
            REPEAT
               write('WHICH CHOICE ? -->');
               read(ch);
               writeln
            UNTIL ch IN ['R','D','r','d'];
            writeln;
            write('ANGLE TO BE CONVERTED -->');
            readln(angle);
            CASE ch OF
               'D','d'  :  angle := (angle/pi)*180.0;
               'R','r'  :  angle := (angle*pi)/180.0
            END;
            writeln;
            write('THE ANGLE IS ',angle,' ');
            CASE ch OF
               'D','d' : writeln('DEGREES');
               'R','r' : writeln('RADIANS');
            END;
            writeln;
            write('ANOTHER CALCULATION? ')
         UNTIL NOT yesorno
    END.
```

Program 9.4 An angles conversion program

9.6 PROBLEMS

9.1 A car requires antifreeze during the winter months (say November to April). Define a set that expresses this.

9.2 Holidays tend to be taken in the summer, at spring time and at Christmas. Define a set of months to express this. How may this set be used to determine before which holidays it is necessary to check that there is antifreeze in the car.

9.3 Write a program to read characters from the keyboard, and count the number of letters (i.e. the characters a to z) that are entered.

9.4 Write a program to read characters for the keyboard, and display only those digits that are entered.

9.5 Write a program that reads characters from the keyboard, and counts the number of

consonants,
vowels,
digits, and
other characters entered.

9.6 Write a program which will read characters from the keyboard, ignore all non-printing characters, and keep a count of each printing character entered. Use the escape key to determine that input has finished, and then display the number of times each character has been entered.

CHAPTER 10
Accessing Collections of Associated Data - Record Structures

10.1 THE NEED FOR RECORD STRUCTURES

As was shown in Chapter 8, arrays are a very useful way of grouping together related information, so long as it is all of the same data type. In general this is what is required when the same information about a number of different objects is to be manipulated. The students' program is a typical example, where the same information is given, i.e. a whole series of marks, about a number of different students. In this chapter the data structures will be looked at that can be used to represent a number of different pieces of information that are known about the same object.

A new compound data structure is required, so that all the information about the object can be stored together. It is necessary to combine a number of different data-types into one, which embraces all the information that is available. This is known as a 'record' structure. In PASCAL, the formal definition is of this form:

```
<record-type> = RECORD
                    <definitions of the data fields>
                END;
```

where each field definition is in the following form:

```
<field-name> : <data-type>;
```

A particular example might help. It is very useful to monitor the petrol consumption of a car. Apart from giving the number of miles travelled, the cost of travelling, etc., a change in the average number of miles travelled per gallon of fuel used is a useful warning indicator of potential problems with the engine. It might be descided that the easiest way of monitoring this would be always to fill the petrol tank, and to keep a record of the date, the amount of fuel, and its cost. It will be possible to work out everything of interest from this information. The date can be stored, most appropriately, as a string, the mileage as an integer, and the total cost, together with the cost per gallon, as real numbers. A suitable data structure to hold this information would therefore be of the type:

```
fillup = RECORD
            date    : alpha;
            mileage : integer;
            cost    : real;
            price   : real
         END;
```

More complex data-structures can be built up, since the definition of each field in the record is not restricted to only the simple data-types that form part of the PASCAL language. This allows very complex structures to be developed, since a field may itself be an array, or even another record. Therefore, in this example, the alpha data-type is the same as that used to store strings in Chapter 8, and must be declared before 'fillup'.

If, for instance, it was decided to store the date as three different data items, the day, the month as a string containing its name, and the year, it would be necessary to redefine the date field as a record. This would make it easier to analyse the petrol consumption on either a monthly or a yearly basis. Suitable TYPE definitions would be:

```
TYPE
   datetype = RECORD
                 day   : 1..31;
                 month : alpha;
                 year  : 0..99
              END;

   fillup   = RECORD
                 date    : datetype;
                 mileage : integer;
                 cost    : real;
                 price   : real
              END;
```

```
VAR
   filling  : fillup;
```

Each field in a record is accessed through the variable record name, followed by the field separated by a decimal point (.). So if a variable 'milestraveled' is to be set to the current mileage, the following would be written:

```
milestraveled := filling.mileage;
```

If, as is often the case, a number of different fields is to be accessed within the same record, a WITH clause can be used of the form:

```
WITH <record-name> DO
   <a compound statement referring to the record fields>
```

within which only the field name need be specified. For example, if all the fields in 'filling' need to be cleared, the following could be written:

```
WITH filling DO
BEGIN
   WITH date DO
   BEGIN
      day := 1;
      month := 'jan';
      year := 0
   END;
   mileage := 0;
   cost  := 0;
   price := 0
END;
```

10.2 COMPLEX VARIABLES

A simple example of where a record structure can be used with advantage, is to represent a complex number. Mathematically there are two ways of writing a complex number. The following form shall be used:

(a + ib)

where a and b are real numbers, a representing the real part, and b the imaginary part, of the complex number. A simple record can be defined to represent this:

```
complex = RECORD
              realpart : real;
              imagpart : real
          END;
```

It is then possible to write a series of procedures to manipulate complex numbers stored in this way.

Let us first consider a program to find the absolute value of a complex number. The program will be required to read in the number, asking the user to type in the real and imaginary parts in turn, calculate the absolute value, which is given by the formula:

$$\text{absolute value} = (\text{realpart}^2 + \text{imagpart}^2)^{1/2},$$

and write out the result. This can be repeated so long as the user has further calculations to perform.

A skeleton program will be of the form:

```
BEGIN
    finished := false;
    REPEAT
        <print heading>
        <read complex number>
        <print out its absolute value>
        <any more calculations ?>
    UNTIL finished
END;
```

A procedure must be used to read in the complex number, since functions can only return values that conform to the built-in simple data types. A suitable procedure heading would therefore be:

```
PROCEDURE cread (VAR c : complex);
```

The absolute value is, however, a real quantity, and can therefore be most appropriately returned as the value of a real function. A suitable function heading would be:

```
FUNCTION cabsolute (c : complex) : REAL;
```

Putting all this together gives program 10.1.

```
PROGRAM complex1(input,output);

TYPE
   complex = RECORD
                realpart : real;
                imagpart :real
             END;

VAR
   cnumber : complex;
   finished : boolean;

PROCEDURE cread(VAR c:complex);

BEGIN
   WITH c DO
   BEGIN
      writeln('ENTER THE COMPLEX NUMBER.');
      write('FIRST, THE REAL PART -->');
      readln(realpart);
      write('NOW, THE COMPLEX PART -->');
      readln(imagpart);
      writeln;
      writeln
   END
END;

FUNCTION cabsolute(c:complex) : real;

BEGIN
   WITH c DO
      cabsolute := sqrt(sqr(realpart)+sqr(imagpart))
END;
```

```
FUNCTION yesorno : boolean;

VAR
   ch : char;

BEGIN
   REPEAT
      read(ch);
      writeln
   UNTIL ch IN ['Y','y','N','n'];
   yesorno := ch IN ['Y','y']
END;

BEGIN
   REPEAT
      page(output);
      writeln;
      write('A PROGRAM TO DETERMINE THE ABSOLUTE VALUE OF A ');
      writeln('COMPLEX NUMBER');
      write('= ========= ========= === ======== ===== == = ');
      writeln('======= ======');
      writeln;
      writeln;
      cread(cnumber);
      writeln('ITS ABSOLUTE VALUE IS ',cabsolute(cnumber));
      writeln;
      writeln;
      write('ANOTHER NUMBER? ');
      finished := NOT yesorno
   UNTIL finished
END.
```

Program 10.1 A program to find the absolute value of a complex number

Mathematical manipulation of complex numbers can also be performed by the use of suitable procedures. Looking, for example, at the addition of two complex numbers,a suitable procedure would take the two arguments, which might be in the form:

(a + ib) and (c + id)

using the formula:

$$(e + if) = ((a + c) + i(b + d))$$

A suitable procedure heading would be:

```
PROCEDURE cadd(arg1,arg2:complex; VAR result : complex);
```

The complete procedure is given as program 10.2.

```
PROGRAM complex1(input,output);

TYPE
   complex = RECORD
                realpart : real;
                imagpart :real
             END;

VAR
   cnumber : complex;
   finished : boolean;

PROCEDURE cread(VAR c:complex);

BEGIN
   WITH c DO
   BEGIN
      writeln('ENTER THE COMPLEX NUMBER.');
      write('FIRST, THE REAL PART -->');
      readln(realpart);
      write('NOW, THE COMPLEX PART -->');
      readln(imagpart);
      writeln;
      writeln
   END
END;
```

```
FUNCTION cabsolute(c:complex) : real;

BEGIN
   WITH c DO
      cabsolute := sqrt(sqr(realpart)+sqr(imagpart))
END;

FUNCTION yesorno : boolean;

VAR
   ch : char;

BEGIN
   REPEAT
      read(ch);
      writeln
   UNTIL ch IN ['Y','y','N','n'];
   yesorno := ch IN ['Y','y']
END;

BEGIN
   REPEAT
      page(output);
      writeln;
      write('A PROGRAM TO DETERMINE THE ABSOLUTE VALUE OF A');
      writeln('COMPLEX NUMBER');
      write('= ======= == ========= === ======== ===== == =');
      writeln('======= ======');
      writeln;
      writeln;
      cread(cnumber);
      writeln('ITS ABSOLUTE VALUE IS ',cabsolute(cnumber));
      writeln;
      writeln;
      write('ANOTHER NUMBER? ');
      finished := NOT yesorno
   UNTIL finished
END.
```

<u>Program</u> <u>10.2</u> A program to add two complex numbers together

10.3 COORDINATE CONVERSION

Another type of data for which record structures can readily be defined are both cartesian and polar coordinates. In both cases it is necessary to store two items of data to locate a point on a two-dimensional surface. In the case of the cartesian coordinate system, these are two distances in the x and the y directions (see figure 10.1). This may be represented by a RECORD, which contains two

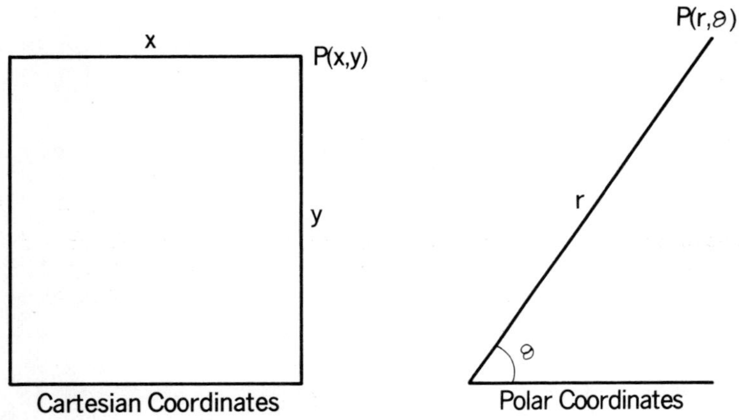

Figure 10.1 The cartesian and polar coordinate systems

fields, one for each of the x and y coordinates:

```
TYPE
   carttype = RECORD
                 x : real;
                 y : real
              END;
```

Polar coordinates, on the other hand, are represented by the distance of the point from the origin, and the angle a line from the origin to the point subtends to a reference line (again see figure 10.1).

This can be represented by a RECORD of the form:

```
polartype = RECORD
               r     : real;
               theta : real
            END;
```

where r represents the distance, and theta the angle.

As with complex numbers, it is possible to manipulate these items by writing suitable procedures. Program 10.3 converts cartesian coordinates into their polar equivalent. First two routines:

```
PROCEDURE readcart(VAR cart : carttype);
```

which reads the cartesian coordinates, and:

```
PROCEDURE writepolar (pol : polartype);
```

which writes out the resulting polar coordinates, are defined. It is then necessary to consider how to carry out the conversion. Another procedure is therefore defined (since PASCAL does not allow structured data types to be returned as the value of a function) that will actually do the conversion:

```
PROCEDURE polar(cart : carttype; VAR pol : polartype);
```

Within this procedure the calculation of the distance of the point from the origin is straightforward, since it is the third side of a right-angled triangle. The angle is not so easy to calculate. There is no problem so long as the point is in the first quadrant. In this case it is only a matter of taking the arctangent. If it is in any other quadrant, however, some further processing is needed to ensure that the right angle is obtained. This is done by the series of conditions at the end of the procedure. The constant 'small' is introduced because real numbers are not stored exactly, within the computer. There must be some degree of approximation, as a continuous band of numbers cannot be represented within a finite number of data bits. If a test is carried out to see whether a given data quantity is exactly zero, the result will only be true if it is stored exactly as zero. It may, however, be stored as a number that is so close to zero as to make no practical difference. If, therefore, a small range is substituted, the condition will trap all the values that would otherwise cause problems.

To avoid any attempt to divide by zero, and thus cause the

procedure to crash when perfectly valid data is passed to it, the situation where a point is exactly on one of the axes is dealt with as a special case by the conditions at the start of the program. The situations that must be trapped in this way are:

(a) When both the x and y coordinates are zero.
(b) When the x coordinate is zero, but the y coordinate is not.

If the point is on the y axis the program will work out the angle correctly.

```
PROGRAM coordinates(input,output);

TYPE
    carttype =  RECORD
                   x : real;
                   y : real
                END;

    polartype = RECORD
                   r : real;
                   theta : real
                END;

VAR
   cartcoord : carttype;
   polarcoord : polartype;
   finished:boolean;
   answer:char;

PROCEDURE readcart(VAR cart : carttype);

BEGIN
   WITH cart DO
   BEGIN
      writeln;
      write('ENTER THE X COORDINATE -->');
      readln(x);
      writeln;
      write('ENTER THE Y COORDINATE -->');
      readln(y)
   END
END;
```

```
PROCEDURE writepolar(pol : polartype);

CONST
   pi = 3.14159;

VAR
   thetadeg : real;

BEGIN
   WITH pol DO
   BEGIN
      writeln;
      writeln('R     = ',r);
      thetadeg := theta*180.0/pi;
      writeln('THETA = ',thetadeg,' DEGREES.')
   END
END;

PROCEDURE polar(cart:carttype;VAR pol:polartype);

CONST
   pi = 3.14159;
   small = 0.00001;

VAR
   xtemp,ytemp : real;

BEGIN
   xtemp := cart.x;
   ytemp := cart.y;
   IF (xtemp>-small) AND (xtemp<small) THEN
      IF (ytemp>-small) AND (ytemp<small) THEN
         BEGIN
            pol.r := 0.0;
            pol.theta := 0.0
         END
      ELSE
         IF ytemp<small THEN
            BEGIN
               pol.r := -ytemp;
               pol.theta := 3*pi/2
            END
         ELSE
```

```
                BEGIN
                   pol.r := ytemp;
                   pol.theta := pi/2
                END
      ELSE
         BEGIN
            xtemp := abs(xtemp);
            ytemp := abs(ytemp);
            pol.r := sqrt(sqr(xtemp)+sqr(ytemp));
            pol.theta := atan(ytemp/xtemp);
            IF (cart.x>=-small) AND (cart.y<=small) THEN
               pol.theta := 2.0*pi-pol.theta
            ELSE
               IF (cart.x<small) AND (cart.y<small) THEN
                  pol.theta := pi+pol.theta
               ELSE
                  IF (cart.x<small) AND (cart.y>-small) THEN
                     pol.theta := pi-pol.theta
         END
   END;

   BEGIN
      REPEAT
         page(output);
         writeln;
         writeln;
         writeln('A PROGRAM TO CONVERT CARTESIAN COORDINATES');
         writeln('          INTO POLAR COORDINATES');
         writeln;
         readcart(cartcoord);
         polar(cartcoord,polarcoord);
         writepolar(polarcoord);
         write('ANOTHER CONVERSION ? (Y/N) -->');
         read(answer);
         writeln;
         IF answer='Y' THEN
            finished:=false
         ELSE
            finished:=true
      UNTIL finished
   END.
```

<u>Program 10.3</u> A program to convert cartesian coordinates to polar coordinates

Program 10.4 is a useful procedure that converts one cartesian coordinate frame to another,given the new origin, and the angle of rotation, in radians. The old coordinates, and the position of the new origin in them are passed as parameters, together with the angle of rotation. The new coordinates are returned.

```
PROCEDURE changecoord (oldcoord,neworigin : carttype;
                       rotation : real;
                       VAR newcoord : carttype);

BEGIN
   WITH newcoord DO
      BEGIN
         x := (oldcoord.x - neworigin.x) * cos(rotation)
              + (oldcoord.y - neworigin.x) * sin(rotation);
         y := (oldcoord.y - neworigin.y) * cos(rotation)
              + (oldcoord.x - neworigin.x) * sin(rotation)
      END
END;
```

Program 10.4 A procedure to convert from one cartesian frame to another

10.4 PROBLEMS

10.1 Write a function to determine the imaginary part of a complex number.

10.2 Write a procedure to subtract two complex numbers.

10.3 Write a procedure to divide two complex numbers.

10.4 Using an array of the fillup records, described in section 10.1, write a program to analyse the petrol consumption of a car, on a monthly basis.

10.5 Write a function that returns the absolute value of a two-dimensional vector.

10.6 Use the procedure 'transform' in program 10.4 as part of a program which converts a series of coordinates into a new frame. It should first ask the user for the coordinates of the new origin, and the rotation. The program should then accept the old coordinates, and display the new ones for each successive point.

10.7 Linear interpolation.

The formula for interpolating a point on a straight line, given two points on the same line, on either side of the desired point is:

$$y = y_1 + \frac{(y_2 - y_1).(x - x_1)}{(x_2 - x_1)}$$

Write a procedure which, given the coordinates of two points on the line, returns the coordinate of the point whose x coordinate has also been passed as a parameter.

CHAPTER 11
Some Further Useful Output Features

11.1 INTRODUCTION

So far the PASCAL compiler has been allowed to print out results in a standard way, that is the system has been left to decide how many decimal places are significant, and allowed it to print them laid out in the best way it could. For simple programs the standard (or default) formats are perfectly adequate. They absolve the programmer from the problem of predicting the size, and form, of the numbers output.

As will have been seen with the output from some of the example programs, however, when more complex program printouts are required, the results can be very untidy, since the computer decides how many characters are necessary to print each number solely on the value to be printed, and not on the numbers printed round it. When a number of different quantities are displayed together, each number is output in the form that is most appropriate to it, but not in any consistent manner. Tables, therefore, do not line up in the way that they would be expected to.

11.2 FORMATTING OUTPUT, PRINTING TABLES, ETC.

PASCAL provides a simple, but powerful, formatting feature, which allows the programmer to define how many characters are to be printed for each number, and for real numbers, the number of places to be printed after the decimal point. This allows the programmer to have complete control over the layout of a program's printout, and with a little practice, to make the computer produce neat and readable reports.

Returning once again to the problem of generating tables of values for square roots, running the programs discussed in section 6.4

certainly generates the appropriate answers, but does not print them out neatly in columns, one under the other. This is not too bad if there are only two columns, and the results are required simply for one's own use. However, if complex tables are required, which will be used by many people, then something with a better appearance is required.

PASCAL does in fact provide quite a sophisticated formatting scheme which, when used with care, allows the programmer to lay out very complex data in the way that he desires. This is done by specifying how many digits are to be printed for any number in the 'write' or 'writeln' statements, immediately following the variable name, separated by a colon. For instance:

```
write(number:6);
```

will print the value of 'number', taking a total of six character positions. If the value of 'number' is small enough not to need six character positions then spaces are printed to the left of it to make up the field. This is sufficient information for the computer to print integers in the desired form. With real numbers, however, it is also necessary to specify how many digits are to be printed after the decimal point. This is done by following the first digit with a colon and a further digit, as for example:

```
write(sum:8:4)
```

states that 'sum' is to be printed in eight character positions, with four digits following the decimal point.

Program 11.1 shows how a table of square roots can be laid out in this way, using FOR loops to specify the columns and rows where each entry is printed. Further 'write' statements are used to print headings so that the computer printout can be used directly.

```
PROGRAM root3(input,output);

CONST
    first=0;
    last =9;
    firstrow=1;
    lastrow=9;
    increment=0.1;
```

```
VAR
   i,base:integer;
   value,sqroot:real;

BEGIN
   page(output);
   writeln;
   writeln('TABLE OF SQUARE ROOTS');
   writeln;
   writeln;
   FOR base := firstrow TO lastrow DO
   BEGIN
      write(base:2,'.0  ');
      FOR i:= first TO last DO
      BEGIN
         value:=base+i*increment;
         sqroot:=sqrt(value);
         write(sqroot:6:3)
      END;
      writeln
   END
END.
```

Program 11.1 A program to print a nicely formatted table of square roots

It is not always the case that the layout of the results is as simple as this, and the next program (program 11.2) illustrates how the format rules can be used to produce a neat layout on the screen. In this case it is the Lunar Lander game. Formatted output is used to give an acceptable display to the player of every data item which is relevant to his next move. Additional 'write' statements are used to print column titles, and to give more information at the start,

```
PROGRAM lunar(input,output);

CONST
   g=6;
   c=32000;
```

```
TYPE
   thrustrange=0..500;

VAR
   fuel,altitude,velocity,acceleration:real;
   thrust:thrustrange;
   reply:char;

BEGIN
     REPEAT
        page(output);
        writeln('   ALT      VEL   FUEL        THRUST');
        writeln('   FEET     FPS   LBS         FOR 10 SECS');
        altitude:=633600.0;  (* 120 MILES UP *)
        velocity:=5280.0;    (* 1 MILE PER SECOND *)
        fuel:=16000.0;
        WHILE (altitude>0) AND (velocity>10) OR (altitude>10) DO
        BEGIN
           write(altitude:9:1,velocity:8:1,fuel:8:1,'    ');
           IF fuel>0 THEN
              readln(thrust)
           ELSE
           writeln;
           fuel:=fuel-5*thrust;
           IF fuel<0 THEN
           BEGIN
              fuel:=0;
              thrust:=0
           END;
           acceleration:=g-thrust*0.55*c/(c+fuel);
           altitude:=altitude-10*(velocity+5*acceleration);
           velocity:=velocity+10*acceleration;
           fuel:=fuel-5*thrust;
           IF fuel<0 THEN
              fuel:=0
       END;
       writeln;
       IF (velocity<10) AND (altitude>-40) THEN
           writeln('GOOD LANDING','FUEL LEFT',fuel:7:1,'LBS')
       ELSE
           writeln('CRASHED',0.1*velocity:7:1,'FEET DEEP');
       writeln;writeln;
```

```
        write('DO YOU WISH TO TRY AGAIN (Y OR N) -->');
        read(reply);
        writeln
      UNTIL reply<>'Y'
   END.
```

Program 11.2 A simple moonlander game

and after the module has landed (or crashed into the moon, as the case may be). Within the program the various control structures are used in such a way that they help the programmer, and anyone else who wishes to read the program, to understand the underlying algorithm used. As the programs become more complicated this is increasingly important, as without an overall concept of what the program is intended to do it is impossible to further develop it, or even to correct errors satisfactorily, since one cannot be certain that any modifications made will not affect other sections of the program.

11.3 DISPLAYING INFORMATION IN THE MOST USEFUL FORM

An extended example of how output can be made much more acceptable by appropriate formatting is given in the mortgage calculation program. Although only two decimal places are meaningful, it is necessary to perform all the calculations using real arithmetic. This means that the results must be rounded before they are displayed. This is performed automatically within PASCAL, as part of the formatting process.

The calculation of the payments needed on a loan is given by the following formula:

$$r = \left[\frac{ip/n}{1 - (1/n + 1)^{-ny}}\right]$$

where r = regular payments
i = annual interest rate
p = principal
n = number of payments per year
y = number of years.

Another common calculation is the principal that can be borrowed for a certain regular repayment. This can be found using the formula:

$$p = \frac{rn}{i}\left[1 - \frac{1}{(1 + i/n)^{ny}}\right]$$

If, on the other hand, it is necessary to calculate the number of years that it will take to repay a loan, at a given level of repayments, this formula can be used:

$$y = \left[\frac{\log(1 - pi/nr)}{\log(1 + i/n)}\right] \cdot \frac{1}{n}$$

Each calculation is performed by a separate procedure, which calls functions to input the information required. Each of these functions checks the data to ensure that it is consistent with the range of values expected. The procedure called is determined by the menu in the main program. If the program is written in this way, it is an easy matter to add further options by modifying the main program and adding the necessary procedures.

The results of each procedure are displayed in a standard form by another procedure, called 'displayresults'. Using just one procedure allows the display to be standardised, so that uniformity is maintained. Since all the information is monetary, it is displayed to two decimal places.

Program 11.3 performs all these calculations.

```
PROGRAM mortgage(input,output);

VAR
   repay,intrate,principal,nopay,noyears : real;
   ch : char;
   finished : boolean;
   setofans : SET OF char;

FUNCTION power(a,b:real) : real;

BEGIN
   IF a <= 0 THEN
      BEGIN
         writeln('YOU CANNOT TAKE THE POWER OF ',a);
         power := 0.0
      END
```

```
   ELSE
      power := exp(ln(a)*b)
END;

FUNCTION readvalue(low,high:real) : real;

VAR
   temp : real;

BEGIN
   write('ENTER A VALUE BETWEEN ',low:6:2,
         ' AND ',high:6:2,' -->');
   readln(temp);
   readvalue := temp;
   writeln
END;

PROCEDURE getprincipal;

CONST
   plow = 0;
   phigh = 30000;

BEGIN
   writeln('ENTER THE PRINCIPAL');
   principal := readvalue(plow,phigh)
END;

PROCEDURE getintrate;

CONST
   ilow = 5;
   ihigh = 25;

BEGIN
   writeln('ENTER THE ANNUAL INTEREST RATE');
   intrate := readvalue(ilow,ihigh)/100
END;

PROCEDURE getnoyears;

CONST
   ylow = 5;
   yhigh = 25;
```

```
BEGIN
   writeln('ENTER THE NUMBER OF YEARS');
   noyears := readvalue(ylow,yhigh)
END;

PROCEDURE getrepayments;

CONST
   rlow = 0;
   rhigh = 500;

BEGIN
   writeln('ENTER THE LEVEL OF REPAYMENTS');
   repay := readvalue(rlow,rhigh)
END;

PROCEDURE getnopayments;

VAR
   ch : char;
   setofans : SET OF char;

BEGIN
   setofans := ['A','Q','M','W'];
   writeln('REPAYMENTS ARE:');
   writeln;
   writeln('     A(NNUAL');
   writeln('     Q(UARTERLY');
   writeln('     M(ONTHLY');
   writeln('     W(EEKLY');
   writeln;
   REPEAT
      write('ENTER SELECTION -->');
      read(ch);
      writeln;
   UNTIL ch IN setofans;
   CASE ch OF
      'A' : nopay := 1;
      'Q' : nopay := 4;
      'M' : nopay := 12;
      'W' : nopay := 52
   END
END;
```

```
PROCEDURE displayresults;

VAR
   ch : char;

BEGIN
   page(output);
   writeln;
   writeln('THE DETAILS OF THE LOAN ARE:');
   writeln;
   writeln('     PRINCIPAL              : ',principal:6:2);
   writeln('     ANNUAL INTEREST RATE : ',
          (intrate*100.0):6:2,'%');
   writeln('     PAYMENTS PER YEAR     : ',nopay:6:2);
   writeln('     NUMBER OF YEARS       : ',noyears:6:2);
   writeln('     REPAYMENT             : ',repay:6:2);
   writeln;write('ENTER <SPACE> TO CONTINUE -->');
   REPEAT
      read(ch)
   UNTIL ch=' '
END;

PROCEDURE calcrepay;

BEGIN
   page(output);
   writeln;
   writeln('CALCULATING THE REPAYMENTS');
   writeln('=========== === ==========');
   writeln;
   writeln;
   getprincipal;
   getintrate;
   getnoyears;
   getnopayments;
   repay := principal/nopay*intrate/(1.0-
            power(((intrate/nopay)+1.0),(-nopay*noyears)));
   displayresults
END;



PROCEDURE calcprincipal;
```

```
BEGIN
   page(output);
   writeln;
   writeln('CALCULATING THE PRINCIPAL');
   writeln('=========== === =========');
   writeln;
   writeln;
   getrepayments;
   getintrate;
   getnoyears;
   getnopayments;
   principal := repay*nopay/intrate*(1.0-1.0/
                power((1.0+intrate/nopay),nopay*noyears));
   displayresults
END;

PROCEDURE calcnoyears;

BEGIN
   page(output);
   writeln;
   writeln('CALCULATING THE TERM OF A LOAN');
   writeln('=========== === ==== == = ====');
   writeln;
   writeln;
   getprincipal;
   getintrate;
   getrepayments;
   getnopayments;
   noyears := -(ln(1.0-principal/repay*intrate/nopay)/
              ln(1.0+intrate/nopay))*1.0/nopay;
   displayresults
END;

PROCEDURE quit;

BEGIN
   page(output);
   finished := true
END;

BEGIN
    setofans := ['R','P','N','Q'];
```

```
    finished := false;
    REPEAT
       page(output);
       writeln;
       writeln('MORTGAGE CALCULATION PROGRAM');
       writeln('======== =========== =======');
       writeln;
       writeln;
       writeln('OPTIONS AVAILABLE ARE');
       writeln('THE CALCULATION OF:');
       writeln;
       writeln('     R(EPAYMENTS');
       writeln('     P(RINCIPAL');
       writeln('     N(O OF YEARS');
       writeln('     Q(UIT');
       writeln;
       write('ENTER SELECTED OPTION -->');
       read(ch);
       IF ch IN setofans THEN
          CASE ch OF
             'R' : calcrepay;
             'P' : calcprincipal;
             'N' : calcnoyears;
             'Q' : quit
          END
    UNTIL finished
 END.
```

Program 11.3 The mortgage calculation program

11.4 PLOTTING GRAPHS

The microcomputer need not output the results of a calculation as just numbers, or text. It may be more appropriate if a graph is produced instead. In its simplest form, the graph may consist of single characters, suitably spaced out on the display. This can be done by arranging for the requisite number of blank spaces to be written before the character that is to form part of the line. Program 11.4 does exactly this by plotting the function:

```
f(x) = exp(-x)*sin(2.0*pi*x)
```

Each line of print represents a small increase in x, and the character positions across the page represent increasing values in y. Dx and dy are the number of character positions that are used to represent a unit distance in each direction. Rx, the value that one line represents, is calculated at the start of the program, before looping over the number of lines to be printed, in this case 32, representing x values between 0 and 1. The program then calculates each value of y and multiplies it by dy, the number of characters used to represent a unit distance along the y-axis. This value must then be rounded to an integer value, to which must be added an offset, y0, which moves the x-axis to the centre of the display. Spaces are then printed across the page to where the character, in this case '*', is printed to represent the value of f(x).

This is adequate to display simple graphs. The scaling must, however, be worked out by the programmer. This is a job that the microcomputer is well suited to perform. A far more general program then results. In addition, a line buffer, which could be defined as a packed array of characters, would allow more than one graph to be plotted on the same axes, together with the inclusion of appropriate axes.

If the graph is to be displayed with the x-axis across the display, rather than down it, as in the previous example, it is necessary to store the plotting area in a page buffer, until all the points have been positioned, and then write the whole graph. This is because the calculation of the points must be performed in the direction of the x-axis, and the plot will be printed in the direction of the y-axis.

```
PROGRAM graph(input,output);

CONST
   dx = 16;
   dy = 32;
   y0 = 20;
   ylim = 32;

VAR
   x,y,rx : real;
   n : integer;
   i : 0..ylim;


FUNCTION f(x:real) : real;
```

```
CONST
   pi = 3.14159;

BEGIN
   f := exp(-x)*sin(2.0*pi*x)
END;

PROCEDURE spaces(numberofspaces:integer);
VAR
   i : integer;

BEGIN
   FOR i:= 0 TO numberofspaces DO
      write(' ')
END;

BEGIN
   rx := 1.0/dx;
   FOR i:=0 TO ylim DO
   BEGIN
      x := rx*i;
      y := f(x);
      n := round(dy*y)+y0;
      spaces(n);
      writeln('*')
   END
END.
```

Program 11.4 A simple graph plotting program

Program 11.5 shows how a buffer of this sort might be used. This buffer must be dimensioned to the current display size. Therefore two constants are used, height, the number of lines that are to be filled by the graph, and width, which is half the line length, less one. This is because it is assumed that the y-axis will be positioned down the centre of the plot. Suitable declarations for the buffer would therefore be:

```
CONST
   width = 19;
   height = 21;
```

```
TYPE
   dx = -width..width;
   dy = 0..height;
   line = PACKED ARRAY [dx] OF char;

VAR
   page : ARRAY [dy] OF line;
```

Another array is also required to store all the data points along the curve to be plotted, until the complete plot can be automatically scaled. For this, a suitable declaration would be:

```
TYPE
   datavect = ARRAY [dx] OF real;

VAR
   datapoints : datavect;
```

It is now possible to start writing the program. First of all the page buffer must be completely cleared to space characters. This will be done by the procedure 'clearpage'. Then the data point must be calculated, and the 'datapoints' vector filled. This is done within the FOR loop. The spacing of these points along the x-axis is controlled by the constant used to convert from x to rx, which is the value used to calculate f(x). Once all the points are calculated, they can be plotted. This is done by the procedure 'plot'. First the 'datapoints' vector is searched for the largest and the smallest values, and a suitable scale factor is calculated. Each data point is multiplied by this scale factor, and the offset from the bottom of the page to the x axis (called y0), is calculated. All this is performed in the procedure 'scale'. The plot then places plotting characters at the right places in the plot buffer. Before the buffer is printed, in 'writepage', the x and the y axes must be added, by 'plotaxes'. The final plot is then displayed.

```
PROGRAM plotgraph(input,output);

CONST
   width = 19;
   height = 21;
```

```
TYPE
   dx = -width..width;
   dy = 0..height;
   datavect = ARRAY[dx] OF real;
   line = PACKED ARRAY[dx] OF char;

VAR
   page : ARRAY[dy] OF line;
   x : dx;
   y : dy;
   datapoints : datavect;
   rx : real;
   yzero : integer;

FUNCTION f(x:real):real;

BEGIN
      IF x=0.0 THEN
         f := 1.0
      ELSE
         f := sin(x)/x
END;

PROCEDURE scale(VAR a:datavect);

CONST
   large = 1.0e30;

VAR
   scalefactor,dmin,dmax : real;
   i : dx;

BEGIN
   dmin := large;
   dmax := -large;
   FOR i:=-width TO width DO
   BEGIN
      IF a[i]<dmin THEN
         dmin:=a[i];
      IF a[i]>dmax THEN
         dmax:=a[i]
   END;
   IF dmax<>dmin THEN
      scalefactor:=height/(dmax-dmin);
```

```
    FOR i:=-width TO width DO
      a[i]:=(a[i]-dmin)*scalefactor;
    yzero := round(-dmin*scalefactor)
  END;

  PROCEDURE clearpage;

  BEGIN
    FOR y:=0 TO height DO
      FOR x:=-width TO width DO
        page[y,x]:=' '
  END;

  PROCEDURE plotaxes;

  BEGIN
    FOR y:=0 TO height DO
      page[y,0] := '.';
    IF yzero IN [0..height] THEN
      FOR x:=-width TO width DO
        page[yzero,x] := '.'
  END;

  PROCEDURE plot(VAR a:datavect;  ch:char);

  VAR
    j : dx;

  BEGIN
    scale(a);
    FOR j:=-width TO width DO
      page[round(a[j]),j] := ch
  END;

  PROCEDURE writepage;

  VAR
    i,j : integer;

  BEGIN
    FOR j:=height DOWNTO 0 DO
    BEGIN
      FOR i:=-width TO width DO
        write(page[j,i]);
```

```
      writeln
    END
  END;

  BEGIN
    clearpage;
    FOR x:=-width TO width DO
    BEGIN
      rx := x*0.40;
      datapoints[x] := f(rx)
    END;
    plot(datapoints,'+');
    plotaxes;
    writepage
  END.
```

Program 11.5 A general graph plotting program, which includes scaling

11.5 PROBLEMS

11.1 Write a program that displays a table of the secants of all the angles from 0 to 20 degrees, in steps of 0.5 degree. Pay particular care to the format of the output.

11.2 Write a program that can be used to balance a cheque book. It should ask for the initial balance, keep an account of salary and other receipts, payments by cheque and on a regular basis, and interest. A running balance should be displayed, and at the end the number of transactions of each type, together with the total of all the transactions.

11.3 Modify the students' marks program in Chapter 8 so as to display a histogram of the number of students in each marks category.

11.4 Write a program to draw graphs of

    f(x) = sin(x)

and

    f(x) = cos(x)

between x=0 and x=2*pi, on the same axes.

11.5 Write a program to read in 100 floating point numbers in the range 0.0 to 10.0 and plot a histogram of the numbers lying in the ranges:

0.0-1.0, 1.0-2.0, 2.0-3.0, ..., 9.0-10.0.

11.6 Plot on a character printer the function

$$y = \frac{x}{(1+x)^3}$$

from x = -3 to x = +4.

At times, this function changes very rapidly. Consider how to ensure that the plot is clear everywhere. (Take particular care in the area around x = -1.)

11.7 One useful type of plot is a density plot in which different characters are used to represent the values of a function at different points. The denser the character, the higher the value at that point.

A suitable range of characters would be:

(space) - + * 0 X.

Produce density plots of the functions

$$z = \sin(x) * \sin(y)$$

and

$$z = \sin(x) + \sin(y).$$

The values of x and y plotted should be

$$\frac{-\pi}{2} <= x <= \frac{\pi}{2}$$

and

$$\frac{-\pi}{2} <= y <= \frac{\pi}{2}.$$

The x axis should run across the page, the y-axis down, and the z-axis up out of the page.

CHAPTER 12
Storing Collections of Related Data - File Structures

12.1 THE NEED FOR FILES

So far, how various types of data are stored within the computer has been looked at, and how programs can be written to manipulate this data in useful ways. All this is very useful, but has a major defect in that all the data collected is lost as soon as the program terminates. This may not be important for simple programs, or when only a little raw data is required, but if the data is to be built up over a series of runs as, for instance, in the case of a cheque book balancing program, or a log of petrol usage, it is very important that the data is stored in an easily accessible form, which can be read back into the computer each time the program is run.

To do this, it is necessary to store the data on some form of backing-storage device, such as a floppy diskette, or possibly, a cassette tape. Most microcomputer users soon find that a large amount of storage is soon required to hold all the information required by their programs. It would be very expensive if it was necessary to provide sufficient floppy-diskette or cassette-tape drives to hold all this information permanently available to the computer. The floppy-diskettes, or cassette-tapes, are, however, in themselves very cheap. Hence the drives are built in such a way that the floppy-diskettes, or the cassette-tapes, can be removed very quickly, and another containing the required information can be inserted in its place. A library of programs, and data, can be built up in much the same way as a music library around a hi-fi system.

With all these different diskettes available the microcomputer must have some means of recognising which are currently loaded into a drive, and thus immediately accessible for the storing and retrieval of information. Before a diskette can be used, a special area is reserved onto which certain information is stored. This area is usually reserved by a special program which forms part of the operating system package, and must be used to initialise the diskette before use.

The exact information which is stored in this area, which is often called the directory, depends on the operating system in use. Typically it would include a name, by which the whole diskette would be recognised (often called the volume identifier) and information on each of the files stored on that volume. The information stored on each file would include not only its name, but also some idea of what sort of information it contains. For instance, whether it contains data, textual information, or the binary code of a program that can be loaded and executed directly. It will also contain information that allows the computer to find the information stored in that file on the diskette. From this it is also possible to determine how much free space is available, and where it is located on the diskette. Other useful information that may be stored is the date that the file was first used, when it was last modified, and possibly when it was last used.

Many microcomputer systems also treat input and output to physical devices as if reading or writing to files with special properties. A printer would therefore be accessed as a file to which individual characters can be written (i.e. the characters are to be printed) but nothing could be read from it (since this would have no meaning). Similarily a special input device, such as a paper-tape reader, can be connected to the microcomputer and accessed as a file of characters that can be read, but not written to, nor can the program stop the reader and start it reading again from the beginning of the tape without the operator physically repositioning the tape.

In PASCAL, files must be declared like any other data type. The declaration must include not only the name of the file, but the type of data that will be contained in each cell. This is done in the following way:

```
VAR
   <fileid> : FILE OF <data type>;
```

where <fileid> is the identifier that is to be used within the program, and <data type> is the type of information that is stored within the file. A file that is to hold a series of integers would therefore be declared as follows:

```
temp : FILE OF integer;
```

In addition many systems require that file identifiers are included in the program heading, so that proper communication can be maintained with the operating system. The standard input and output units are already included at the start of the program, to which must now be added any additional files used. This is done in the program statement, which now has the form:

```
PROGRAM <program name>(<file identifiers>);
```

and for our example would look like this:

```
PROGRAM fileex(input,output,temp);
```

12.2 FILE MANIPULATION

Before a file can be used, it must first be opened, that is, the physical copy of the file must be located on the backing store, the file indexes must be checked for consistency, and a file buffer, that holds the next few items in the file readily accessible in the microcomputer's memory, must be filled. This initialisation is performed by one, of two, special routines, depending on whether the file is to be written to, as well as read from, or read from only. These routines are:

```
rewrite(<file identifier>);
```

if the file is to be written to, and:

```
reset(<file identifier>);
```

if the file is only to be read from. It should, however, be noted that once a file has been written to, information cannot be read from it, until it has been 'reset' (or 'rewritten').

Once all the information has been read from, or written to the file, a certain amount of housekeeping is required to ensure that everything in the buffer is written to the file, an end-of-file marker is placed at the very end, and the operating system disconnects the file from the program and updates its file indexes so that it is permanently stored. Another standard procedure is provided to do this:

```
close(<file identifier>);
```

which should be used whenever a file is finished with, whether 'reset' or 'rewrite' was used to open it.

The information held in files is stored in a special way, which reflects the way in which files are used within a computer system. A file is considered to consist of a series of identical storage cells, each of which can contain one item of the type specified when the file is declared. Although the precise way that this is stored on a floppy-diskette, or a cassette-tape, depends on the type of medium used, the mechanism can be represented in the following way. The microcomputer maintains a file pointer, which marks the next cell in the file, either to be read from, or written to, and a buffer which contains the last item read, or the next item to be written to the file, as figure 12.1 shows.

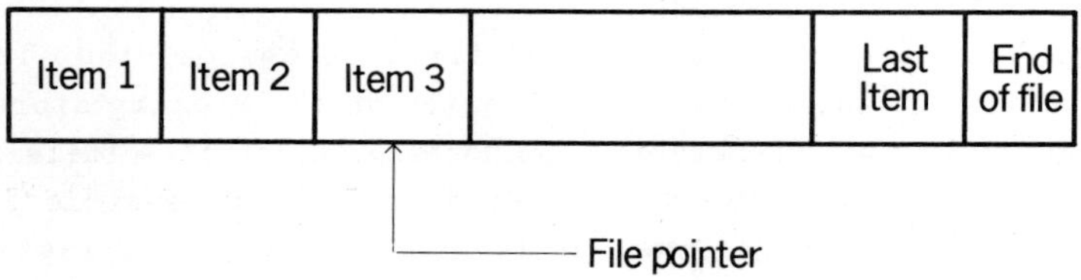

Figure 12.1 File organisation

When either reading from, or writing to, a file, the programmer must first of all fill the buffer, and then either use that information within the program, or write it out to the file. This is done with two program statements. For instance, when reading information from a file, the file pointer must first be updated, and the data read into the buffer. It may then be read by the program, and be manipulated as required.

This is programmed in the following way:

```
get(<fileid>);
<variable> := <fileid>^;
```

First, the contents of the next cell available on the file must be read into the buffer, and the pointer updated. This is performed by the standard procedure 'get'. Once this has been done the contents of the buffer can be used as any other variable of the relevant data type.

As an example, the following code could be used to input a character from the standard input device, known to the program as INPUT (this is usually the microcomputer keyboard).

```
get(input);
ch := input^;
```

These two commands would perform the same function as:

```
read(ch);
```

Output is handled in a similar way, except that the data to be written to the file must first be placed in the buffer, and then written to the file medium. This is done by using the standard procedure 'put', as follows:

```
<fileid>^ := <expression>;
put(<fileid>);
```

For example, the following would output the character held in the variable, ch, to the principal output device, known as OUTPUT (this is usually the microcomputer display):

```
output^ := ch;
put(output);
```

and would be equivalent in operation to:

```
write(ch);
```

There is also a useful routine 'eof' which can be used to tell whether all the information in a file has been read, or not. It has the form:

```
eof(<fileid>)
```

and returns a boolean value, true, if there is no further information to be read, and false, otherwise. It can be used, for instance, as the terminating condition in a REPEAT loop to ensure that all the information in a file has been processed. A suitable program skeleton would be:

```
REPEAT
   <process items held in file>
UNTIL eof(<fileid>);
```

This is a very powerful construction, and will be used in most of the programs discussed in this chapter.

Program 12.1 is a simple illustration of how files work. The file 'temp' is declared to be a file of integers, into which is to be written 100 numbers. This is done within the procedure 'writefile'. 'Temp' must be opened for the first time using 'rewrite', rather than 'reset', because data is going to be written into the file, and not just read from it. The data items are then written to the file from within the loop, as has already been seen. Once all the data has been written, it can be closed, thus ensuring that the end of file is marked with a special record that the microcomputer operating system will recognise later.

The file can now be read back, and its contents checked by displaying the values found on the display. The procedure 'readfile' does this. First the file must be reopened. This is done using the 'reset' procedure, since this time the file is only being read from. A repeat loop is then used to read the numbers, and display them. Initially the standard function 'eof(temp)' will give a value of false. The loop is therefore repeated until a special end-of-file record is read in, and recognised by the operating system. The next time that 'eof(temp)' is called it will return a value of true. The loop will then terminate. The order in which a copy of the contents of the buffer is made, and the next value read in, using 'put(temp)' should also be noted. When the file is opened, using either 'reset' or 'rewrite', the first item is always read into the buffer. In other words a 'get(temp)' is automatically performed. If another 'get(temp)' were executed before the buffer had been read, the first data item in the file would have been lost. Once all the data items have been read, the file is closed, and the program exits.

```
PROGRAM fileex(input,output,temp);

VAR
   temp : FILE OF integer;
   i,j : integer;

PROCEDURE writefile;

BEGIN
   rewrite(temp);
```

```
    FOR i:=1 TO 100 DO
    BEGIN
      temp^:=i;
      put(temp)
    END;
    close(temp)
  END;

  PROCEDURE readfile;

  BEGIN
    reset(temp);
    REPEAT
      j:=temp^;
      get(temp);
      writeln(j)
    UNTIL eof(temp);
    close(temp)
  END;

  BEGIN
    page(output);
    writeln('STARTING TO WRITE FILE');
    writefile;
    writeln;
    writeln('FINISHED WRITING FILE');
    writeln;
    writeln('READING FILE BACK');
    readfile;
    writeln;
    writeln('END OF PROGRAM ... ');
  END.
```

Program 12.1 A program to write 100 integers out onto a file

A more useful program is program 12.2. When the average of a series of readings is required, it is often necessary to reprocess the data several times to obtain the final results required, rejecting information which is obviously invalid. The best way to do this is to store the data in a file, which can be read as many times as necessary. Program 12.2 allows the user to enter data into a file, display it for checking, and calculate the average and the standard deviation, rejecting data outside of predefined limits.

Not only is this program useful when considering the effect of changes in the acceptance limits, but it can also be used for many other applications, where the mean of only part of the data is required. It may be, for example, that the mean of the lowest 50% of the data is the most significant statistic. This program allows this to be found very easily. First the mean of all the data is calculated, and then the mean of the lowest half of the data is found by rejecting any data with a value above that mean.

```
PROGRAM meanoffile(input,output,data);

TYPE
   datafile = FILE OF real;

VAR
   ch       : char;
   finished : boolean;
   data     : datafile;

FUNCTION yesorno : boolean;

VAR
   ch : char;

BEGIN
   REPEAT
      read(ch);
      writeln
   UNTIL ch IN ['Y','y','N','n'];
   yesorno := ch IN ['Y','y']
END;

PROCEDURE waitforsp;

VAR
   sp : char;

BEGIN
   write('ENTER <SPACE> TO CONTINUE');
   REPEAT
      read(sp)
   UNTIL sp=' '
```

```
END;

PROCEDURE readdata;

VAR
   dataitem : real;
   noitems  : integer;

BEGIN
   page(output);
   writeln;
   writeln('ENTERING DATA ...');
   writeln;
   rewrite(data);
   noitems := 0;
   REPEAT
      write('ENTER NEXT DATA ITEM -->');
      readln(dataitem);
      data^ := dataitem;
      put(data);
      noitems := noitems+1;
      write('IS THERE ANY MORE DATA (Y/N) -->')
   UNTIL NOT yesorno;
   writeln(noitems:4,' DATA ITEMS HAVE BEEN ENTERED');
   close(data);
   waitforsp
END;

PROCEDURE quit;

BEGIN
   finished := true;
   page(output)
END;

PROCEDURE meanofdata;

VAR
   lowerlimit,upperlimit  : real;
   sumdata,sumdatasq      : real;
   nodataitems,norejected : integer;
   item                   : real;
```

```
    FUNCTION rejected : boolean;

     BEGIN
        IF (item<lowerlimit) OR (item>upperlimit) THEN
           rejected := true
        ELSE
           rejected := false
     END;

     PROCEDURE rejlimits;

     BEGIN
        writeln;
        write('ENTER LOWER LIMIT -->');
        readln(lowerlimit);
        write('ENTER UPPER LIMIT -->');
        readln(upperlimit);
        writeln
     END;

     PROCEDURE displaymean;

     VAR
        mean,stdev : real;
        noused     : integer;

     BEGIN
        page(output);
        writeln;
        writeln('LOWER REJECTION LIMIT - ',lowerlimit:6:2);
        writeln('UPPER REJECTION LIMIT - ',upperlimit:6:2);
        writeln;
        writeln('NUMBER OF DATA ITEMS READ - ',nodataitems:4);
        writeln('NUMBER REJECTED           - ',norejected:4);
        noused := nodataitems-norejected;
        writeln('NUMBER USED               - ',noused:4);
        writeln;
        mean := sumdata/noused;
        stdev := sqrt((sumdatasq-(sqr(sumdata)/noused))/(noused-1));
        writeln('MEAN               - ',mean:6:2);
        writeln('STANDARD DEVIATION - ',stdev:6:2);
        waitforsp
     END;
```

```
BEGIN
   reset(data);
   page(output);
   writeln;
   writeln('CALCULATING MEAN AND STANDARD DEVIATION');
   rejlimits;
   nodataitems := 0;
   sumdata := 0.0;
   sumdatasq := 0.0;
   norejected := 0;
   REPEAT
      item := data^;
      get(data);
      nodataitems := nodataitems+1;
      IF NOT rejected THEN
         BEGIN
            sumdata := sumdata+item;
            sumdatasq := sumdatasq+sqr(item)
         END
      ELSE
         norejected := norejected+1
   UNTIL eof(data);
   displaymean;
   close(data)
END;

BEGIN
   finished := false;
   REPEAT
      page(output);
      writeln;
      writeln('A PROGRAM TO CALCULATE THE MEAN');
      writeln('AND STANDARD DEVIATION OF DATA');
      writeln('HELD IN A FILE.');
      writeln;
      writeln('     R(EAD DATA');
      writeln('     C(ALCULATE MEAN');
      writeln('     Q(UIT');
      writeln;
      write('SELECT OPTION -->');
      read(ch);
      writeln;
```

```
          IF ch IN ['R','C','Q'] THEN
             CASE ch OF
                'R' : readdata;
                'C' : meanofdata;
                'Q' : quit
             END
       UNTIL finished
    END.
```

Program 12.2 A program to calculate the mean of data held in a file

12.3 TEXT FILES

One type of file is so common that special facilities are provided within PASCAL, so that this type can be handled much more easily than any other. This type of file contains just characters, and is called a text file. Special versions of the standard procedures 'read', 'write', 'readln' and 'writeln' are provided, to which has been added an extra parameter, the file identifier. These procedures are used in exactly the same way as the simpler forms when information is to be read from the keyboard, and the results displayed on the screen. A special file type, 'text', has also been provided as part of the language, to assist the programmer. Examples of its use, assuming the declaration:

```
VAR
   textfile : text;
```

are:

```
read(textfile,a,b,c,d);
write(textfile,'this is a message');
readln(textfile,x,y,z);
```

and

```
writeln(textfile,'the answer is :- ',ans:6:2);
```

In addition to 'eof', there is another function, 'eoln', that only has meaning in relation to text files. It is used to test whether the end of a line has been reached. It, too, returns a boolean value, true, if the file pointer is at the end of a line, and false, otherwise. It has the form:

eoln(<fileid>)

and is used in exactly the same way as 'eof'.

One very useful housekeeping program is to copy the contents of one file to another. Program 12.3 is one such program for copying text files. After opening both files, it reads characters from the source

```
PROGRAM copy(input,output,infile,outfile);

VAR
    inchar:char;
    infile,outfile:text;

PROCEDURE openinputfile(VAR f:text);

    (* SEE TEXT FOR DESCRIPTION *)

PROCEDURE openoutputfile(VAR f:text);

    (* SEE TEXT FOR DESCRIPTION *)

PROCEDURE closefiles(VAR f,g:text);

    (* SEE TEXT FOR DESCRIPTION *)


BEGIN
    page(input);
    writeln('    PROGRAM TO COPY FILES.');
    writeln;
    writeln;
    openinputfile(infile);
    openoutputfile(outfile);
    REPEAT
        REPEAT
            read(infile,inchar);
            write(outfile,inchar)
        UNTIL eoln(infile);
        writeln(outfile)
    UNTIL eof(infile);
```

```
        closefiles(input,output);
        page(output)
    END.
```

Program 12.3 A program to copy text from one file to another.

file, and immediately writes them out again to a destination file. Once the end of the source file has been found (using 'eof'), both files are closed, and the program terminates. It is necessary to include a test for 'eoln', and to use 'writeln' to write the last character on each line to the destination file, to ensure that the proper markers for each line end are recorded on the file medium.

This program also illustrates another problem. The PASCAL file opening procedures were designed for use on large computers, where all programs would be entered into a job well, and run at some later time, when their turn came. It is therefore assumed that the computer's operating system will link the file identifiers, listed in the program heading, with physical files that it has available to it. On microcomputers, this way of working is, at best, an absolute nuisance, and at worst, absolutely impossible, since the program is run immediately the user issues the necessary command. There is no need for an extensive, and very costly, operating system to manage the available resources, and ensure that two programs are not trying to make use of the same facilities, be it peripherals, such as printers or card readers, or files. There is therefore no facility available to pick up the program heading and allocate the required files to their related file identifiers. Most microcomputer PASCALs resolve this problem by requiring the programmer to provide additional information to the file-opening procedures 'reset', and 'rewrite', and to close, so that the program knows what it is expected to do with the file once it is no longer to be used. Needless to say, each compiler deals with this problem in a different way. They all, however, provide the same basic amenity of issuing the physical filename that the operating system recognises, from within the program. To show how this can be used most effectively, Appendix B gives examples of three procedures written in UCSD PASCAL, which can be rewritten for use with most of the other compilers:

openinputfile(VAR f:text)	reads name of the file to be read from the keyboard, and prepares it for reading.
openoutputfile(VAR f:text)	reads the name of the file to

	be written to, and opens it for writing.
closefiles(VAR f,g:text)	closes both files. Assumes that f has been used only for reading from, and g has been written to.

It should be noted that when a file parameter is passed to a procedure, it must always be preceded by VAR, even if information is only to be read from it. This is because the file pointer still requires updating. These procedures have been used in program 12.3.

12.4 PROGRAMS THAT MANIPULATE TEXT

It is usual for most reasonable disk-based operating systems to provide their own facility to copy the contents of a file to another. Since this facility is written with a knowledge of the internal workings of the system, it is likely to be much faster than program 12.3. What the system designer cannot do, except to a very limited extent, is to provide the means to manipulate the text as it is copied from one file to another.

In this section, four programs will be looked at that process the text as it is transferred. The first is a simple program which removes spaces (used for indenting the lines in a PASCAL program) from the start of each line. This can be very useful if a special formatting program is available which will lay the program out in a standard form. There are a number of these programs in circulation, and all of them work best if there is no original indentation to confuse them. If the text of a program is run through this program first, then all original indentation is removed, so enabling the formatting program to be started from scratch. The program, program 12.4, is exactly the same as program 12.3, except that every character after a new line is tested, and discarded, until a non-space character is found.

```
PROGRAM spaces(input,output,infile,outfile);

VAR
    inchar:char;
```

```
        infile,outfile:text;

    PROCEDURE openinputfile(VAR f:text);

        (* SEE TEXT FOR DESCRIPTION *)

    PROCEDURE openoutputfile(VAR f:text);

        (* SEE TEXT FOR DESCRIPTION *)


    PROCEDURE closefiles(VAR f,g:text);

        (* SEE TEXT FOR DESCRIPTION *)


    PROCEDURE skipspaces;

    VAR
        ch:char;

    BEGIN
        REPEAT
           read(infile,ch);
           IF eoln(infile) THEN
               writeln(outfile)
        UNTIL ch<>' ';
        write(outfile,ch)
    END;

    BEGIN
        page(input);
        writeln('    PROGRAM TO REMOVE INDENTATION FROM');
        writeln('                 PASCAL PROGRAMS.');
        writeln;
        writeln;
        openinputfile(infile);
        openoutputfile(outfile);
        REPEAT
            skipspaces;
            REPEAT
                read(infile,inchar);
                write(outfile,inchar)
            UNTIL eoln(infile);
```

```
        writeln(outfile);
    UNTIL eof(infile);
    closefiles(infile,outfile);
    page(output)
END.
```

Program 12.4 A program to remove the indentations from a PASCAL program

Program 12.5 uses the upper-case to lower-case function discussed in Chapter 9, to convert all the characters in a file to lower-case. It uses the same skeleton as the other two programs, but passes each character through the conversion routine, before dispatching it to the destination file. This program is particularly useful when using those machines that do not allow lower case characters to be input directly from the keyboard, but is capable of storing the full ASCII character set in memory.

```
PROGRAM uppertolower(input,output,infile,outfile);

VAR
    inchar,ch:char;
    infile,outfile:text;

PROCEDURE openinputfile(VAR f:text);

    (* SEE TEXT FOR DESCRIPTION *)

PROCEDURE openoutputfile(VAR f:text);

    (* SEE TEXT FOR DESCRIPTION *)

PROCEDURE closefiles(VAR f,g:text);

    (* SEE TEXT FOR DESCRIPTION *)

FUNCTION convert(ch:char):char;

VAR
   i:integer;
```

```
    BEGIN
       IF ch IN ['A'..'Z'] THEN
          BEGIN
             i:=ord(ch);
             i:=i+32;
             convert:=chr(i)
          END
       ELSE
          convert:=ch
    END;

    BEGIN
        page(input);
        writeln('    PROGRAM TO CONVERT CHARACTERS FROM');
        writeln('            UPPER TO LOWER CASE');
        writeln;
        writeln;
        openinputfile(infile);
        openoutputfile(outfile);
        REPEAT
            REPEAT
                read(infile,inchar);
                ch:=convert(inchar);
                write(outfile,ch)
            UNTIL eoln(infile);
            writeln(outfile)
        UNTIL eof(infile);
        closefiles(infile,outfile);
        page(output)
    END.
```

Program 12.5 A program to convert all upper-case characters to lower-case

Another manipulative program is program 12.6, which can be used to delete comments from a program. On most microcomputer implementations, comments start with the characters '(*' and '*)'. Since these characters can be used in other contexts, it is necessary to determine that they are next to each other before they can be accepted as comment delimiters. In addition, most compilers accept compiler directives which allow the programmer to select various options during compilation. These can include controls on the listing of the program, the ability to include sections of the program held in other files, so that the program text can be broken up into smaller files for easier editing, and controlling what checks, if any, will be included in the final object code. It is usual to be able to select whether code will be included to check for errors in subscripts, errors in file handling, and arithmetic overflow, since the extra code required can slow the program down considerably. These directives are also included as comments, but have a '$' as the first character to indicate their purpose. In most cases, these form an essential part of the program, and must be left. It is therefore necessary to distinguish between the different states the program can be in:

(a) copying characters, but looking for a '(' to indicate the possible start of a comment.
(b) after finding a '(', the next character must be a '*' for this to be a comment, otherwise the '(' and the present character must be copied over, and the program must start looking for a '(' again.
(c) after finding a '(*', if the next character is a '$', all three characters must be copied over, and the program set back into copying mode again.
(d) once in a comment, all characters are ignored until a '*' is found, which might signal its end.
(e) once a '*' has been found in a comment, if the next character is a ')', otherwise the program must go back and look for the next '*'.

These program states are best defined in a suitable CASE statement, so that each action can be defined independently.

```
PROGRAM remcomments(input,output,infile,outfile);

VAR
    infile,outfile:text;

PROCEDURE openinputfile(VAR f:text);

    (* SEE TEXT FOR DESCRIPTION *)

PROCEDURE openoutputfile(VAR f:text);

    (* SEE TEXT FOR DESCRIPTION *)
```

```
PROCEDURE closefiles(VAR f,g:text);

    (* SEE TEXT FOR DESCRIPTION *)


PROCEDURE removecomments(VAR f,g:text);

VAR
   ch:char;
   state:(copying,foundopenbr,incommand,incomment,foundstar);

BEGIN
   state:=copying;
   WHILE NOT eof(f) DO
      IF eoln(f) THEN
      BEGIN
         readln(f);
         IF state=copying THEN
            writeln(g)
      END
      ELSE
      BEGIN
         read(f,ch);
         CASE state OF

         copying      : IF ch='(' THEN
                           state:=foundopenbr
                        ELSE
                           write(g,ch);

         foundopenbr  : IF ch='*' THEN
                           state:=incommand
                        ELSE
                           BEGIN
                              write(g,'(',ch);
                              state:=copying
                           END;
         incommand     : IF ch='$' THEN
                           BEGIN
                              write(g,'(*$');
                              state:=copying
                           END
                          ELSE
```

```
                    state:=incomment;

    incomment     : IF ch='*' THEN
                      state:=foundstar;

    foundstar     : IF ch=')' THEN
                      state:=copying
                    ELSE
                      state:=incomment

    END
  END
END;

BEGIN (* OF MAIN PROGRAM *)
    page(input);
    writeln('    PROGRAM TO REMOVE COMMENTS FROM');
    writeln('           PASCAL PROGRAMS.');
    writeln;
    writeln;
    openinputfile(infile);
    openoutputfile(outfile);
    removecomments(infile,outfile);
    closefiles(infile,outfile);
    page(output)
END.
```

Program 12.6 A program to remove all comments from a PASCAL program, apart from those which start as compiler directives

The final program in this section (program 12.7) can be used to differentiate between PASCAL keywords, and other words, by changing them into upper-case, and changing the rest to lower-case. It is a development of program 12.6. Again a series of possible situations was defined:

(a) the normal state of copying each character as it is read. Certain characters must be looked for, however. '(' starts a comment if the next character is a '*' and ''' starts a quoted string. Any character starts a symbol.

(b) within a comment all characters are left strictly alone.

(c) within a quoted string all characters are left strictly alone.

(d) a symbol consists of letters and digits. It is therefore terminated by the first non-alphanumeric character. A lookup table is provided to test whether it is a keyword or not. If it is, it is copied as an upper-case character, otherwise lower-case.

In this program, the furthest that it is necessary to look ahead is one character, so a special character read routine, 'readch', is

```
PROGRAM printprog(input,output,infile,outfile);

CONST
    nkeywords=36;
    strlngth=15;
    eol=13;

TYPE
    str=PACKED ARRAY[1..strlngth] OF char;

VAR
    infile,outfile:text;
    key:ARRAY[1..nkeywords] OF str;
    setofalph:SET OF char;
    setofnum:SET OF char;
    setofanum:SET OF char;
    word:str;
    wptr:0..strlngth;

PROCEDURE openinputfile(VAR f:text);

    (* SEE TEXT FOR DESCRIPTION *)

PROCEDURE openoutputfile(VAR f:text);

    (* SEE TEXT FOR DESCRIPTION *)

PROCEDURE closefiles(VAR f,g:text);

    (* SEE TEXT FOR DESCRIPTION *)
```

```
PROCEDURE setup;

BEGIN
   key[ 1] := 'AND             ';key[ 2] := 'ARRAY           ';
   key[ 3] := 'BEGIN           ';key[ 4] := 'CASE            ';
   key[ 5] := 'CONST           ';key[ 6] := 'DIV             ';
   key[ 7] := 'DO              ';key[ 8] := 'DOWNTO          ';
   key[ 9] := 'ELSE            ';key[10] := 'END             ';
   key[11] := 'FILE            ';key[12] := 'FOR             ';
   key[13] := 'FORWARD         ';key[14] := 'FUNCTION        ';
   key[15] := 'GOTO            ';key[16] := 'IF              ';
   key[17] := 'IN              ';key[18] := 'LABEL           ';
   key[19] := 'MOD             ';key[20] := 'NIL             ';
   key[21] := 'NOT             ';key[22] := 'OF              ';
   key[23] := 'OR              ';key[24] := 'PACKED          ';
   key[25] := 'PROCEDURE       ';key[26] := 'PROGRAM         ';
   key[27] := 'RECORD          ';key[28] := 'REPEAT          ';
   key[29] := 'SET             ';key[30] := 'THEN            ';
   key[31] := 'TO              ';key[32] := 'TYPE            ';
   key[33] := 'UNTIL           ';key[34] := 'VAR             ';
   key[35] := 'WHILE           ';key[36] := 'WITH            '
END;

PROCEDURE readch(VAR f:text;VAR ch,nextch:char);

BEGIN
   ch:=nextch;
   IF eoln(f) THEN
      BEGIN
         readln(f);
         nextch:=chr(eol)
      END
   ELSE
      read(f,nextch)
END;

FUNCTION convert(ch:char):char;

BEGIN
   IF ch IN ['A'..'Z'] THEN
      convert:=chr(ord(ch)+32)
   ELSE
      convert:=ch
END;
```

```
PROCEDURE printsymbol(word:str;keysymbol:boolean;VAR g:text);

VAR
   i:integer;
   ch:char;

BEGIN
   i:=1;
   WHILE (i<=strlngth) AND (word[i]<>' ') DO
      BEGIN
         IF keysymbol THEN
            write(g,word[i])
         ELSE
            BEGIN
               ch:=convert(word[i]);
               write(g,ch)
            END;
         i:=i+1
      END
END;

PROCEDURE writesymbol(word:str;VAR g:text);

VAR
   i:integer;
   keysymbol:boolean;

BEGIN
   keysymbol:=false;
   FOR i:=1 TO nkeywords DO
      IF word=key[i] THEN
         keysymbol:=true;
   printsymbol(word,keysymbol,g)
END;

PROCEDURE print(VAR f,g:text);

VAR
   ch,nextch:char;
   state:(copying,insymbol,instr,incomment);

BEGIN
   state:=copying;
```

```
read(f,nextch);
WHILE NOT eof(f) DO
BEGIN
   readch(f,ch,nextch);
   CASE state OF

   copying      : BEGIN
                     IF ch='(' THEN
                        BEGIN
                           IF nextch='*' THEN
                              state:=incomment;
                           write(g,ch)
                        END
                     ELSE
                        IF  ch=''''THEN
                           BEGIN
                              state:=instr;
                              write(g,ch)
                           END
                        ELSE
                           IF ch IN setofalph THEN
                              BEGIN
                                 word:='                  ';
                                 state:=insymbol;
                                 word[1]:=ch;
                                 wptr:=1;
                              END
                           ELSE
                              write(g,ch);
                  END;

   incomment     : BEGIN
                     IF (ch='*') AND (nextch=')') THEN
                        state:=copying;
                     write(g,ch)
                   END;

   insymbol      :  BEGIN
                      IF NOT (ch IN setofanum) THEN
                         BEGIN
                            state:=copying;
                            writesymbol(word,g);
                            write(g,ch)
                         END
```

```
                                    ELSE
                                       BEGIN
                                          IF wptr=strlngth THEN
                                             BEGIN
                                                writesymbol(word,g);
                                                wptr:=0;
                                                word:='              ';
                                             END;
                                          wptr:=wptr+1;
                                          word[wptr]:=ch
                                       END;
                                 END;

            instr          :     BEGIN
                                   IF ch='''' THEN
                                      state:=copying;
                                      write(g,ch)
                                 END
               END
            END
      END;

      BEGIN (* OF MAIN PROGRAM *)
          word:='              ';
          setofalpha:=['A'..'Z'];
          setofnum:=['0'..'9'];
          setofanum:=setofalpha+setofnum;
          setup;
          page(input);
          writeln;
          writeln;
          writeln('    PROGRAM TO PRINT UCSD PASCAL PROGRAMS');
          writeln('           IN A NEATER FORMAT');
          writeln;
          openinputfile(infile);
          openoutputfile(outfile);
          print(infile,outfile);
          closefiles(infile,outfile);
          page(output);
      END.
```

<u>Program</u> <u>12.6</u> A program to reformat a PASCAL program, so that keywords are in capital letters, and user-defined names are in small letters

provided that returns ch, the current character and nextch, the next character. It is often useful to do this where only a one-step look-ahead is required, as otherwise the number of possible states can become unwieldy.

12.5 PROBLEMS

12.1 In a typical experiment, three different readings are taken every minute. Write a program which records each set of readings in a file, and displays them for checking once all the data has been entered.

12.2 Write another program that will calculate the mean and standard deviation of each of the three sets of readings recorded in the last problem.

12.3 It is often necessary to filter out obviously inconsistent data. Rewrite the last program so that before processing the data, the maximum and minimum acceptable values can be set. If any data item falls outside its acceptance limits, all three data items recorded for that reading should be rejected. Display the number of rejections with the averages.

12.4 Another common way of analysing data is to fit it to a straight line, i.e a function of the form:

$$f(x) = ax + b.$$

The parameters a and b can be calculated according to the least squares method, using the formulae:

$$a = \frac{\sum x_i^2 \sum y_i - \sum x_i \sum x_i y_i}{n \sum x_i^2 - \sum x_i \sum y_i}$$

and

$$b = \frac{n \sum x_i y_i - \sum x_i \sum y_i}{n \sum x_i^2 - \sum x_i \sum y_i}$$

where n is the number of data points.
Write a program that reads the x and y coordinates from the keyboard, and stores them in a file. It should then calculate the parameters of the best line that can be drawn through them.

The following commands should be supported:

N)ew File
A)dd More Data
F)it Data
L)ist Data Items.

12.5 Write a program to read the characters entered from the keyboard, and store them in a text file.

12.6 Write a program that reads the text file written in the last exercise, and displays its contents on the screen.

12.7 Write a program that reads a PASCAL program, and puts spaces on each side of the symbol ':='. How would you change your program to take account of spaces that are already there?

12.8 Write a program which will list a text file, dividing it into pages, and heading each page with the page number and a title.

CHAPTER 13

The Use of PASCAL to Write Programs for Small Controller-type Microcomputer Applications

13.1 INTRODUCTION

So far, the programs that have been looked at have manipulated data, of different types, within the microcomputer, or transferred it to, or from, files held on some special backing store device, such as a floppy-disk drive. It is the intention in this chapter to look at some of the programming problems encountered when trying to collect data directly, from the real world, and making the microcomputer control special events directly. Even though all data used as input to a computer program must represent some facet of the real world, it must be extracted, and summarised in a form in which it can be input into the microcomputer by the person wishing to use it. This is often a long and tedious job.

For this sort of application only a fraction of the power of even the smallest microprocessor is usually required, so it would be very wasteful of precious resources to use a fully configured system for such an application. A very small system with just enough memory to store the program and any working data needed, together with all the necessary input and output devices required, would be quite sufficient. If, in addition, the program was stored in read-only memory, and written so as to start running as soon as the power was turned on, no complex initialisation process would be required, and indeed it would appear that no microcomputer was there at all.

There are a number of different ways in which the microcomputer can be used to monitor and control other equipment. These include:

(a) The monitoring of readings from test instruments, and their storage, ready for analysis by another program, once all the readings have been collected. This can save considerable effort, where, previously, someone had to sit and record each reading as it was taken. The program can be so written to take readings at a predetermined time interval, or when the microcomputer senses that some event of special interest is happening.

(b) The control of a particular function, or series of functions, which would be awkward to perform in any other way. It may, for instance, require a number of actions to start some process, all performed in a set order, and according to a closely specified time sequence. To do this manually might require considerable training, and would still be prone to mistakes. A microcomputer would have no difficulty in performing these tasks in the correct order, as soon as a single button were pressed.

(c) The microcomputer can take readings from sensors, and decide, itself, what action is needed, depending on what it finds.

In this chapter, programs will be looked at that may be used to solve simple examples of all three types of application.

When considering how to program controller-type programs, it will immediately be realised that there are no statements in PASCAL which allow the programmer to communicate directly with the hardware interfaces that actually read data into the computer system, and send the signals that are interpreted by external circuitry, to control motors, lights, or other useful circuitry. This is because every application is different, and requires special handling. There will be a different number of inputs and outputs, and they will be configured in different ways, to suit the application, making it impossible to design standard phrases that can be used by the programmer to say what action is required. It is therefore necessary to write the parts of the program that actually communicate directly with the hardware in some other language. Most microcomputer PASCAL compilers allow procedures and functions, which have been written in the microcomputer's assembly language, to be linked to the main PASCAL program before it is run. It is then only necessary to specify the procedure, or function, heading as part of the PASCAL program, and write the actual code in assembler, which does allow direct access to all the hardware facilities of the machine.

In the place of the body of the procedure, or function, to be added later, a special keyword, EXTERNAL, is used. As an example, a function to read a switch setting (TRUE for on, and FALSE for off) would have as a suitable heading:

```
FUNCTION switch(switchno:integer) : boolean;
EXTERNAL;
```

It is a good principle to write in assembler only those parts of the program that require direct access to the hardware of the machine. All the rest of the program can be perfectly well written in PASCAL. This makes the program much easier to read, and understand.

13.2 SWITCHES AND LIGHTS

It is now possible to look at a simple example. First, the equipment to which the microcomputer is connected must be specified. In this case some of the programs that can be written to make use of eight switches and eight lights (see figure 13.1) will be looked at. Each switch and light is assigned an identification number from 0 to 8. External routines can then be defined to read the switches, and to

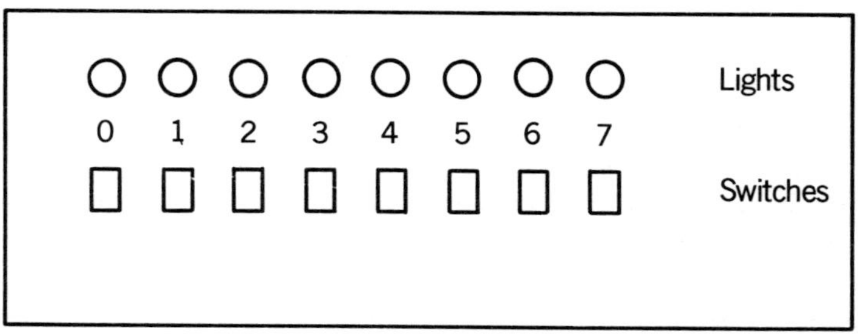

Figure 13.1 A switch and light box

turn the lights on and off. Suitable definitions might be:

```
TYPE
   switchno = 0..8;
   lampno = 0..8;
   lampstatus = (on,off);
```

```
FUNCTION switch(no:switchno) : boolean;
EXTERNAL;

PROCEDURE lamp(no:lampno;status:lampstatus);
EXTERNAL;
```

In addition, it is necessary to initialise the interface, setting each line to an input, or an output, and to set all the lights off. Another routine is therefore required:

```
PROCEDURE initialise;
EXTERNAL;
```

All these routines will have to be written in assembler, and linked to the PASCAL program before it can be executed.

The first example gives the program needed to light the lamps one after the other, in turn. A simple loop over all the lamps is all that is required. If this loop is contained within another which loops continuously, the lamps will continue flashing so long as the program runs:

```
initialise interface

REPEAT
   loop over all lamps
   wait
   light lamp
   wait again
   turn lamp off
   end of loop
UNTIL false;
```

It is often necessary to program delays into control programs, either because the equipment that the microcomputer is attached to cannot perform its required action rapidly enough, or because the microcomputer works so fast that, if there was no delay, it would be impossible to see what action was being taken. In this case, for instance, if no delays were included, the lamps would flash so rapidly that they would not be seen. Program 13.1 gives the complete program.

```
PROGRAM flash(input,output);

CONST
   maxlampno = 7;
   period = 500;

TYPE
   lampno = 0..maxlampno;
   lampstatus = (on,off);

VAR
   i : lampno;

PROCEDURE initialise;
EXTERNAL;

PROCEDURE lamp(no:lampno; status:lampstatus);
EXTERNAL;

PROCEDURE turnlampsoff;

VAR
   i : lampno;

BEGIN
   FOR i:=0 TO maxlampno DO
      lamp(i,off)
END;

PROCEDURE wait(waittime:integer);

VAR
   i,j,k : integer;

BEGIN
   FOR i:=0 TO waittime DO
      FOR j:=0 TO waittime DO
         k := i+j
END;
BEGIN
   initialise;
   turnlampsoff;
   REPEAT
      FOR i:=0 TO maxlampno DO
```

```
        BEGIN
           wait(period);
           lamp(i,on);
           wait(period);
           lamp(i,off)
        END
     UNTIL true
   END.
```

Program 13.1 The light flashing program

It is also possible to arrange for the lamps to light in response to the settings of the related switch. A suitable skeleton for this would therefore be:

```
initialise interface

REPEAT
   loop over all lamps and switches
      if switch is on
         turn lamp on
      otherwise
         turn lamp off
   end of loop
UNTIL false
```

The complete program is given as program 13.2.

```
PROGRAM swandlamp(input,output);

CONST
   maxswandlampno = 7;

TYPE
   swandlampno = 0..maxswandlampno;
   lampstatus = (on,off);

VAR
   i : swandlampno;

PROCEDURE initialise;
EXTERNAL;
```

```
PROCEDURE lamp(no:swandlampno;
               status:lampstatus);
EXTERNAL;

FUNCTION switch(no:swandlampno) : boolean;
EXTERNAL;

BEGIN
   initialise;
   REPEAT
      FOR i:=0 TO maxswandlampno DO
      BEGIN
         IF switch(i) THEN
            lamp(i,on)
         ELSE
            lamp(i,off)
      END
   UNTIL true
END.
```

Program 13.2 A program to read switches, and turn the corresponding lights on

13.3 CONTROLLING A SMALL D.C. MOTOR

Another interesting problem is the control of a small electric motor, of the sort used to power many models. It may, for instance, be necessary to arrange for it to accelerate slowly to a predetermined speed, either forward, or backward. Over the years many conventional circuits have been developed as controllers, which make the motor

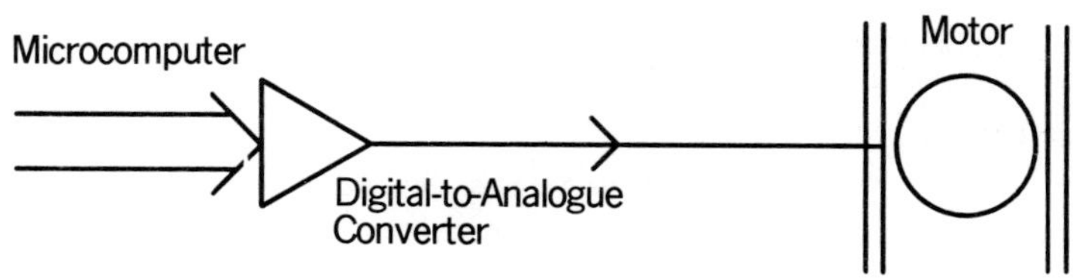

Figure 13.2 The motor control circuit

behave in this way. The advantage of introducing a microcomputer is, however, that the motor control can be integrated into a totally automated control system.

If the speed is controlled by a digital-to-analogue converter, which accepts numbers in the range 0 to 255 (0 being stationary, and 255, full speed), very fine control can be exercised. The motor control procedure might have a heading of the following type:

```
TYPE
   speedrange = 0..255;
   directions = (forward,reverse);

PROCEDURE motor(speed:speedrange;way:directions);
EXTERNAL;
```

A suitable program would read a maximum speed from the keyboard, and then read three control push buttons. When the first is pressed, the motor will move forward, the middle one will stop it, and the third will make it move in reverse. The motor will accelerate, and decelerate, at a predefined rate, controlled by the program. It should be noted that, with the use of a microcomputer, the acceleration and deceleration rates can all be different, something that would be quite difficult to arrange using conventional circuitry. It is also desirable to arrange that once the motor starts running, it must be stopped before it can be restarted in the opposite direction, otherwise unfortunate accidents might result.

What then would the program look like? After initialising the interface, it asks for the maximum speed to be typed in. It then waits for either the forward or the reverse key to be pressed, and then speeds the motor to the desired speed. Once this speed is reached, it waits for the stop button to be pressed, when it slows down to a stop, and then waits for one of the direction buttons to be pressed. The skeleton looks like this:

```
initialise interface
read in maximum speed

REPEAT
   wait for forward or reverse button  to be pressed
   start motor in the desired direction
   wait for stop button to be pressed
   stop motor
UNTIL false
```

The complete program is program 13.3.

```
PROGRAM motorcontrol(input,output);

CONST
   maxswno    = 7;
   period     = 100;
   normswitch = 0;
   revswitch  = 1;

TYPE
   switchno   = 0..7;
   speedrange = 0..255;
   directions = (normal,reverse);

VAR
   speed : speedrange;
   way   : directions;

PROCEDURE motor(speed:speedrange; way:directions);
EXTERNAL;

FUNCTION switch(no:switchno) : boolean;
EXTERNAL;

PROCEDURE initialise;
EXTERNAL;

PROCEDURE wait(waittime:integer);

VAR
   i,j,k : integer;

BEGIN
   FOR i:=0 TO waittime DO
      FOR j:=0 TO waittime DO
         k := i+j
END;

PROCEDURE startmotor(speed:speedrange;
                     VAR way:directions);
```

```
VAR
   switchset : boolean;
   i         : speedrange;

BEGIN
   page(output);
   writeln;
   writeln('TURN SWITCHES ON TO START');
   writeln('           SWITCH 0 = NORMAL');
   writeln('           SWITCH 1 = REVERSE');
   switchset := false;
   REPEAT
      IF switch(normswitch) THEN
         BEGIN
            switchset := true;
            way := normal
         END
      ELSE
         IF switch(revswitch) THEN
            BEGIN
               switchset := true;
               way := reverse
            END
   UNTIL switchset;
   FOR i:=0 TO speed DO
   BEGIN
      motor(i,way);
      wait(period)
   END
END;

PROCEDURE stopmotor(speed:speedrange;
                    way:directions);

VAR
   i : speedrange;
   switchreset : boolean;

BEGIN
   page(output);
   writeln;
   writeln('RESET DIRECTION SWITCH, TO STOP MOTOR');
   switchreset := false;
```

```
      REPEAT
         IF way=normal THEN
            IF NOT switch(normswitch) THEN
               switchreset := true
         ELSE
            IF NOT switch(revswitch) THEN
               switchreset := true
      UNTIL switchreset;
      FOR i:= speed-1 DOWNTO 0 DO
         BEGIN
            motor(i,way);
            wait(period)
         END
   END;

   BEGIN
      page(output);
      writeln;
      writeln('MOTOR CONTROL PROGRAM.');
      writeln('===== ======= =======');
      writeln;
      writeln;
      write('ENTER MAXIMUM SPEED (0..255) -->');
      readln(speed);
      initialise;
      REPEAT
         startmotor(speed,way);
         stopmotor(speed,way)
      UNTIL true
   END.
```

Program 13.3 The motor control program

13.4 TEMPERATURE CONTROL

Another interesting problem is where the microcomputer is attached to an electric heater, which is being used to warm something to which is attached a thermocouple thermometer. The microcomputer is also attached to the thermocouple. Figure 13.3 illustrates a typical example of this sort of system.

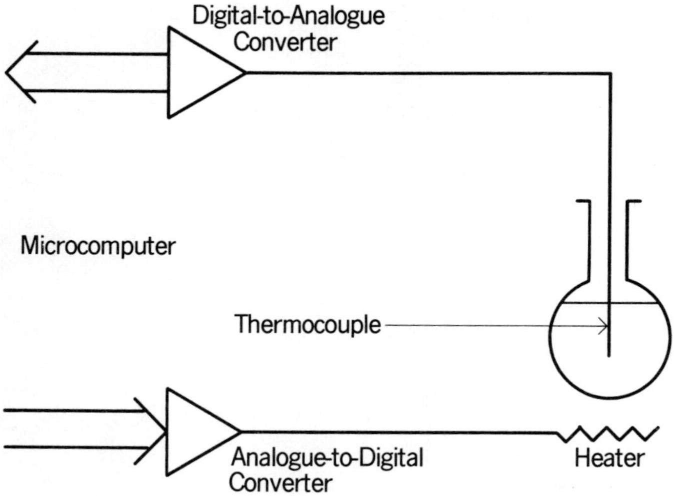

Figure 13.3 A temperature control experiment

The heater can be turned on and off by the computer, so that a suitable procedure might be:

```
TYPE
   action = (on,off);

PROCEDURE heater(turning:action);
EXTERNAL;
```

The temperature reading is, however, a little more complicated. The thermocouple must be connected to an analogue-to-digital converter, which generates a number that is proportional to the temperature reading. The thermocouple does not, however, represent the reading in any normal temperature units, as might be read from a conventional thermometer. This reading must be scaled to give a value that is, for instance, in degrees celsius, before it is of any real use to us within the program. This can be quite a complicated arithmetic process, and as such, is more appropriately written in PASCAL. The main part of the scaling program might be written in PASCAL, leaving only the probe-reading part in assembler. This might then look something like:

```
FUNCTION temperature : real;

CONST
   offset = 10;
   scale = 0.5;

FUNCTION probe : integer;
EXTERNAL;

BEGIN
   temperature := offset+scale*probe
END;
```

A typical application for this type of system would be to keep a temperature within some predefined range. This might be done with a program of the form:

```
initialise interface
read in lower and upper temperature range

REPEAT
   read temperature
   if temperature is above range
      make sure that the heater is off
   otherwise
      if temperature is below range
          make sure that the heater is on
UNTIL false
```

The completed program is program 13.4.

```
PROGRAM tempcontrol(input,output);

TYPE
   action = (on,off);

VAR
   lowerlim,upperlim : real;
   temp : real;
```

```
PROCEDURE initialise;
EXTERNAL;

PROCEDURE heater(turning:action);
EXTERNAL;

FUNCTION probe : integer;
EXTERNAL;

FUNCTION temperature : real;

CONST
   offset = 10.0;
   scale  = 0.5;

BEGIN
   temperature := offset+scale*probe
END;

PROCEDURE readtrange;

BEGIN
   page(output);
   writeln;
   write('ENTER THE LOWER TEMPERATURE LIMIT -->');
   readln(lowerlim);
   write('ENTER THE UPPER TEMPERATURE LIMIT -->');
   readln(upperlim)
END;

BEGIN
   readtrange;
   initialise;
   page(output);
   writeln;
   REPEAT
      temp := temperature;
      writeln('CURRENT TEMPERATURE - ',temp:6:2);
      IF temp >= upperlim THEN
         heater(off)
      ELSE
```

```
        IF temp <= lowerlimit THEN
           heater(on)
     UNTIL false
  END.
```

Program 13.4 Keeping a temperature between set limits

Sometimes it is necessary to keep the temperature as close as possible to some predefined value. This could be done with program 13.4 by setting the upper and lower limits as close as possible, above and below the required temperature. With this program the temperature is still outside these limits for a fair proportion of the time, because the heater is only turned on, and off, once they have been reached. A more satisfactory procedure would be to vary the heater power, so that as the temperature reaches its required value, the amount of heating decreases. In this way a very fine control can be exercised. The interface, however, only allows the heater to be turned on and off. What can be done is to pulse it, making the pulses longer as the temperature drops below its required value. This can be performed perfectly well by a procedure of the form:

```
PROCEDURE pulse(pulselength:0..15);

CONST
    waittime = 10;

VAR
    i : integer;

BEGIN
    heater(on);
    FOR i:=0 TO 15 DO
    BEGIN
        IF i=pulselength THEN
            heater(off);
        wait(waittime)
    END
END;
```

Thus a pulse length of 0 effectively turns the heater off, and a pulse length of 15 effectively keeps it on all the time. The wait is required so that the total time taken by the loop is long enough for the heater to have time to warm to whatever it is supposed to. The constant 'waittime' should be adjusted to allow this to happen. A suitable program would therefore look like this:

```
initialise interface
read in desire temperature

REPEAT
   read temperature
   if less than that required
      calculate offset
      pulse heater
   otherwise
      leave heater off
UNTIL false
```

The offset must be scaled to an integer in the range 0 to 15. A suitable range might be for the heater to be left on almost continuously if the temperature is more than two degrees less than that required. This is what is done in program 13.5.

```
PROGRAM propcontrol(input,output);

CONST
   pulsewait = 150;
   maxpulse = 15;

TYPE
   action = (on,off);
   pulserange = 0..maxpulse;

VAR
   temp : real;
   inttemp,tempdiff : real;
   plength : pulserange;

PROCEDURE initialise;
EXTERNAL;

PROCEDURE heater(turning:action);
EXTERNAL;
```

```
FUNCTION probe : integer;
EXTERNAL;

FUNCTION temperature : real;

CONST
   offset = 10.0;
   scale  = 0.5;

BEGIN
   temperature := offset+scale*probe
END;

PROCEDURE wait(waiting:integer);

VAR
   j,k,l : integer;
BEGIN
   FOR j := 0 TO waiting DO
      FOR k := 0 TO waiting DO
         l := 1
END;

PROCEDURE pulse(pulselength:pulserange);

CONST
   waittime = 10;

VAR
   i : integer;

BEGIN
   heater(on);
   FOR i := 0 TO maxpulse DO
      BEGIN
         IF i=pulselength THEN
            heater(off);
         wait(waittime)
      END
END;

PROCEDURE readtemp;

BEGIN
```

```
      page(output);
      writeln;
      write('ENTER INTENDED TEMPERATURE -->');
      readln(inttemp)
   END;

   BEGIN
      initialise;
      readtemp;
      writeln;
      REPEAT
         temp := temperature;
         writeln('CURRENT TEMPERATURE - ',temp:6:2);
         IF temp<inttemp THEN
            BEGIN
               tempdiff := inttemp-temp;
               IF tempdiff>3.0 THEN
                  plength := maxpulse
               ELSE
                  plength := round(tempdiff*5.0);
               pulse(plength)
            END
         ELSE
            wait(pulsewait)
      UNTIL false
   END.
```

Program 13.5 Proportional control

It is impossible, in a short chapter such as this, to more than scratch the surface of what is becoming a major use of microprocessors and microcomputers. All that can be done is to show some of the interesting possibilities offered by this type of application. In the past this has been considered by programmers and computer scientists to be something of a black art, but with the widespread availability of cheap LSI interface chips, this is no longer so. Designing and building interfaces is not difficult, and there are now many books that tell you how this can be done.

13.5 PROBLEMS

13.1 Write a program to flash the eight lamps as increasing binary digits.

13.2 Write a program that would read three switches as a binary digit, and light that lamp.

13.3 Write a program that sets the speed of a motor by reading the value of a potentiometer through an analogue-to-digital converter. The direction is set by a switch. What is the advantage of using a microcomputer for this purpose?

13.4 A particular application requires an electric motor to start a certain time after the start button has been pressed, and for it not to be stopped for another set time. Write a program that can be used to control the motor.

APPENDIX A

The ASCII Character Set

CODE DEC	CODE HEX	CHAR	CODE DEC	CODE HEX	CHAR	CODE DEC	CODE HEX	CHAR	CODE DEC	CODE HEX	CHAR
0	00	NUL	32	20	SPACE	64	40	%	96	60	`
1	01	SOH	33	21	!	65	41	A	97	61	a
2	02	STX	34	22	"	66	42	B	98	62	b
3	03	ETX	35	23	£	67	43	C	99	63	c
4	04	EOT	36	24	$	68	44	D	100	64	d
5	05	ENQ	37	25	%	69	45	E	101	65	e
6	06	ACK	38	26	&	70	46	F	102	66	f
7	07	BEL	39	27	'	71	47	G	103	67	g
8	08	BS	40	28	(	72	48	H	104	68	h
9	09	HT	41	29	)	73	49	I	105	69	i
10	0A	LF	42	2A	*	74	4A	J	106	6A	j
11	0B	VT	43	2B	+	75	4B	K	107	6B	k
12	0C	FF	44	2C	,	76	4C	L	108	6C	l
13	0D	CR	45	2D	-	77	4D	M	109	6D	m
14	0E	SO	46	2E	.	78	4E	N	110	6E	n
15	0F	SI	47	2F	/	79	4F	O	111	6F	o
16	10	DLE	48	30	0	80	50	P	112	70	p
17	11	DC1	49	31	1	81	51	Q	113	71	q
18	12	DC2	50	32	2	82	52	R	114	72	r
19	13	DC3	51	33	3	83	53	S	115	73	s
20	14	DC4	52	34	4	84	54	T	116	74	t
21	15	NAK	53	35	5	85	55	U	117	75	u
22	16	SYN	54	36	6	86	56	V	118	76	v
23	17	ETB	55	37	7	87	57	W	119	77	w
24	18	CAN	56	38	8	88	58	X	120	78	x
25	19	EM	57	39	9	89	59	Y	121	79	y
26	1A	SUB	58	3A	:	90	5A	Z	122	7A	z
27	1B	ESC	59	3B	;	91	5B	[	123	7B	{
28	1C	FS	60	3C	<	92	5C	\	124	7C	¦
29	1D	GS	61	3D	=	93	5D	]	125	7D	}
30	1E	RS	62	3E	>	94	5E	^	126	7E	~
31	1F	US	63	3F	?	95	5F	_	127	7F	DEL

APPENDIX B

Example Procedures to Open Files Under Program Control in UCSD PASCAL

The original definition of PASCAL was written when nearly all programs were compiled, and run, on large computers, having been entered on punched cards. The whole job, including not only the program and the data which it was required to process, but also the instructions to the computer as to how it was to perform this task, were all read in together, and stored on backing storage, until there was sufficient processor time and memory available to run it. If there were too many jobs for the computer to process immediately, a queue developed, and each took its turn to be processed. Once the program had been run, any output was also stored on backing storage until the right printer was available for it to be printed out. The person running the program had no idea of when it was going to run, and therefore had to provide all the data that was necessary, either as part of the job, or in pre-existing files, held on backing store.

Since, on a large computer, several jobs were likely to be active at the same time, it was necessary to make file handling and manipulation a function of the computer's operating system, so that unfortunate clashes in use between different jobs trying to use the same files could be avoided. When a program required access to a file, it would have to send a special message to the operating system, saying so, and whether it wished to read and write information to it, or just read from it. The file would then be reserved for the use of that job. Standard PASCAL maintains this system, by requiring the programmer to list as part of the program heading, all the file identifiers that are to be used. For instance:

```
PROGRAM example(input,output,temp);
```

says that the program will use the standard input file, the standard output file, and another file, to be called 'temp'. As standard PASCAL has been designed, it is then for the operating system to associate these file identifiers with the actual files that are to be used.

When writing programs which are intended to be run on microcomputers, there is usually no complex operating system to do all this work for you. There is also, normally, only one program active, and therefore many of the problems on larger systems are just not going to occur. The file handling is dealt with by special routines that are always in memory, and can therefore be called directly from the program. Most compilers have been written so that these routines can be called through the normal PASCAL file-handling statements. It is, however, necessary to provide extra information to the file-opening procedures 'reset' and 'rewrite'. This is usually in the form of the name of the file, as known to the operating system, so that the proper relationship can be established.

This facility can be used, simply, to open specifically named files, or in a more general way, to allow any user of the program to specify the file on which he wishes it to act. This appendix gives three procedures (programs B1, B2 and B3), written in UCSD PASCAL, as examples of how this may be done. UCSD PASCAL has a large number of extensions to the PASCAL standard, many of which have been specifically designed to ease the programmer's task in an interactive environment. The extensions used within these procedures are:

(a) The UCSD compiler has an additional data type, 'string', which can be read, and written directly.

(b) Both 'reset' and 'rewrite' take an additional parameter of type 'string', which contains the filename of the file to be used.

(c) Special procedures are available to manipulate strings. Specifically:

'pos' takes as parameters a character, and a string, and returns the position of the character in the string, if present, and 0 otherwise.

'concat' takes two strings as parameters, and returns the concatonated string, in the first parameter.

(d) It is possible to stop a fatal error occurring, using the I compiler option. That is:

(*$i-*) turns the error checking off

and

(*$i+*) turns it back on again.

Example Procedures To Open Files Under Program Control In UCSD PASCAL

```
PROCEDURE openinputfile(VAR f:text);

VAR
    fname:string;

BEGIN
    (*$I-*)
    REPEAT
       writeln('TYPE "!" FOR THE SYSTEM WORKFILE');
       write('INPUT FILE -->');
       readln(fname);
       IF pos('!',fname)=1 THEN
           fname:='*SYSTEM.WRK.TEXT'
       ELSE
           IF pos('.',fname) = 0 THEN
               fname := concat(fname,'.TEXT');
       reset(f,fname)
    UNTIL ioresult = 0;
    (*$I+*)
    writeln(fname,' OPEN FOR READING')
END;
```

<u>Program B.1</u> A procedure to open a file for reading in UCSD PASCAL

While the error checking is turned off, a special function, 'ioresult', can be used to check the result of the last input or output operation. If 'ioresult' returns a value of zero, then the operation was successful.

```
PROCEDURE openoutputfile(VAR f:text);

VAR
   fname:string;

BEGIN
   (*$I-*)
   REPEAT
      write('OUTPUT FILE -->');
      readln(fname);
```

```
        rewrite(f,fname)
    UNTIL ioresult = 0;
    (*$I+*)
    writeln(fname,' OPEN FOR WRITING')
  END;
```

Program B.2 A procedure to open a file for writing in UCSD PASCAL

(e) There is an additional, optional, parameter to the 'close' command, which tells the operating system whether a file created by the program is to be stored permanently, or not. If 'lock' is present, it will be kept, and if it is not the file will be lost as soon as it is closed (see program B.3).

```
PROCEDURE closefiles(VAR f,g:text);

BEGIN
   close(f,lock);
   close(g,lock)
END;
```

Program B.3 Closing files in UCSD PASCAL

These facilities are also available on most other microcomputer PASCAL systems, but because of their non-standard nature, will not, necessarily, look quite the same. It should not prove to be difficult to write procedures which duplicate their function.

APPENDIX C

Some Differences Between UCSD PASCAL and Standard PASCAL

UCSD PASCAL differs from standard PASCAL, as defined in 'The PASCAL User Manual and Report' (second edition) by Kathleen Jensen and Nicklaus Wirth (Springer-Verlag 1975). Many of the differences are in the use of files and input/output in general, as well as the addition of STRING variables. These features are described, as far as they are needed for the examples in this book, in Appendix B. For further information the reader is refered to the documentation that is provided with the UCSD system.

This appendix is intended to provide a reference list of those items that are significantly different in UCSD PASCAL from the accepted standard. These include:

a. The CASE statement.

In standard PASCAL an execution error is generated when there is no label equivalent to the selection variable in the CASE statement. UCSD PASCAL does not generate this execution error, but passes on to the first statement following the CASE statement, without selecting any of the options within it. This simplifies the writing of programs since complex tests to ensure that the selection variable is set to one of the expected values are not required. If, for instance, a simple menu is required which allows the user to select between three options (say 'a', 'b' and 'c'), each of which is implemented by means of a procedure, the following code could be used in UCSD PASCAL:

```
      .
      .
  accepted := false;
  REPEAT
     displaymenu;
     read(ch);
```

```
        CASE ch OF
           'a' : optiona;
           'b' : optionb;
           'c' : optionc
       END
     UNTIL accepted;
        .
        .
```

So long as each of the procedures called by the CASE statement sets the boolean variable 'accepted' to true before returning, this section of code will keep displaying the menu until an acceptable option is selected.

b. Comments.

UCSD PASCAL supports two forms of the comment bracket:

```
    {                          }
and
    (*                        *)
```

Once entered, the comment is terminated by the related opposing bracket (that is the two types of bracket cannot be mixed in the same comment). This allows sections of program text that include comments to be bracketed out by using brackets of the other type. Nested comments are not recognised as such by the compiler.

c. The GOTO Statement.

There is an unconditional jump statement in standard PASCAL, of the form:

```
GOTO <label>
```

where 'label' is an unsigned integer, which must be defined in a label declaration of the form:

```
LABEL <list of labels>
```

immediately following the program or procedure heading in which it is to be used.

UCSD PASCAL supports a far more limited form of the GOTO statement than does standard PASCAL. Before GOTO can be used a special compiler option must be turned on with the compiler option:

```
(*$G+*)
```

UCSD also requires that the label to be jumped to must be in the same procedure block as the GOTO statement. Since the principal use of the GOTO statement in standard PASCAL is to jump out of a procedure on finding that things have gone disastrously wrong, this is not a particularily useful feature.

d. The new standard procedure 'exit'.
This new standard procedure takes as its only parameter a procedure or function name, and when executed leaves it immediately, and returns to the calling program. Thus:

```
exit(proc)
```

will exit immediately from 'proc' (and any procedures called within it) and return to the program or procedure that called it. It should be noted that if 'proc' is a function, its value will be undefined unless a suitable assignment has been made before 'exit' was called.

There is a special form of 'exit':

```
exit(program)
```

which allows the programmer to terminate execution and return control to the operating system at any point within the program.

e. Packed arrays.
The standard PASCAL procedures:

pack

and

unpack

are not provided in UCSD PASCAL. Arrays are packed and unpacked automatically, as required.

f. Program headings.
In UCSD PASCAL the file list in the program heading is optional, and is not used by the compiler. The linkage with real file names, as recognised by the microcomputer's operating system, is performed by 'reset' and 'rewrite' (see Appendix B).

Thus:

```
PROGRAM test(input,outpt,temp);
```

and

```
PROGRAM test;
```

are equivalent.

g. Segment procedures.
The small amount of memory that is available on most microcomputer systems means that many large programs cannot be fitted in. UCSD PASCAL provides the means of splitting the program into 'segments' which are loaded into memory one after the other, rather than all at the same time. This is a form of 'overlaying'. Any procedure or function may be turned into a 'segment' by adding the keyword SEGMENT at the beginning of the heading, for example:

```
SEGMENT PROCEDURE initialise;
```

and

```
SEGMENT FUNCTION principal(repay,noyears,nopay:real):real;
```

All segments must be declared before any other statements that generate code. There may be a maximum of seven segments, including the main program.

h. Sets.
In UCSD PASCAL sets may have up to 4080 elements. Set comparisons are allowed so long as the base type of each is the same, or both are subranges of the same base type.

i. Extended comparisons.
The two comparison operators:

```
=
```

and

```
<>
```

have been extended to include comparisons between two arrays of compatible types.

j. Long integers.
Integers in UCSD PASCAL are usually stored in a single 16-bit word, allowing a range of values from -32827 to +32828. For

some applications this is very restricting, so an additional type called 'long integer' is provided. All the usual integer operators (+, -, *, DIV, MOD, unary + and unary -) are supported, and long integers can be used in structured data types anywhere that an integer is legal.

Long integers are declared by adding a positive integer, giving the maximum number of digits required, in square brackets, after the reserved word INTEGER in the declaration. Thus:

```
VAR
   long : INTEGER[12];
```

declares the variable 'long' to be of type long integer which can store a number of up to 12 digits.

When constants are declared to have values outside the range of normal integers, they are automatically stored as long integers.

Two additional standard procedures are provided to allow the conversion of long integers to other data types. To convert a long integer, 'long' to a standard integer the standard procedure:

```
trunc(long)
```

is used. If long is greater than MAXINT an error results. A long integer can be converted to a UCSD string 'str' using the procedure:

```
str(long,str)
```

where str will contain a string consisting of the digits forming the number stored in int.

k. Units.

UCSD PASCAL makes provision for including pre-compiled libraries of useful procedures and functions, known as 'units', within a user's program. Each unit consists of an 'interface' that contains all the data types, variables, constants, procedures and function headings that can be used from within the user's program, and an 'implementation' part which includes everything that is strictly local to the unit.

To make the procedures and functions in a unit available within a program its name must appear in a special statement between the program heading and the first declarations. The form of this statement is:

```
USES <list of units to be used>;
```

For example:

```
PROGRAM example;
USES wonderstuff;
```

allows the programmer to use any procedures or functions in 'wonderstuff' within his program.

Further Reading

This book is intended to give an informal introduction to programming in PASCAL. It is not intended to give a formal definition of the language, or the facilities offered within it. For a detailed definition of the language, the reader is referred to:

Jensen and Wirth. PASCAL User Manual and Report. Springer-Verlag. (1975)

Other books that will be found of use include:

Zaks. An Introduction to PASCAL, including UCSD PASCAL. Sybex. (1980)
Findley and Watt. PASCAL, An Introduction to Methodical Programming. Pitman. (second edition 1981)
Welsh and Elder. Programming in PASCAL. Prentice-Hall. (1979)
Grogono. Programming in PASCAL. Addison-Wesley. (revised 1980)

Several books deal specifically with UCSD PASCAL, and the facilities provided by that system:

Bowles. A Beginner's Guide to UCSD PASCAL. Byte Books. (1980)
Bowles. Microcomputer Programming using UCSD PASCAL. Springer-Verlag. (1977)
Clark. UCSD p-System and UCSD Pascal Users' Manual. Softech Microsystems. (Second Edition 1981).
Clark and Koehler. The UCSD Pascal Handbook. A Reference and Guidebook for Programmers. Prentice-Hall. (1982)

More general books on programming in PASCAL are:

The BYTE Book of PASCAL. Byte Books. (1979)
Miller. PASCAL Programs for Scientists and Engineers. Sybex. (1981)

Books on structured programming include:

Introductory

Program Design. Byte Books. (1978)
Meek and Heath. Guide to Good Programming Practice. Ellis Horwood. (1980)

Advanced

Dahl *et al.* Structured Programming. Academic Press. (1972)
Alagic and Arbib. The Design of Well-Structured Programs. Springer-Verlag. (1978)

The main text book on the definition and use of data structures is:

Wirth. Algorithms + Data Structures = Programs. Prentice-Hall. (1976)

also

Cole. A Structured Programming Approach to Data. Macmillan. (1978)

Another very useful book, which describes many facilities that are commonly required in programs is:

Kernighan and Plauger. Software Tools in PASCAL. Addison-Wesley. (1981)

Answers to Selected Problems

3.1

yes	no
yes	no
no	yes
no	yes
no	no
yes	yes

3.2

```
PROGRAM first(output);

BEGIN
   page(output);
   writeln('THIS IS MY FIRST PASCAL PROGRAM')
END.
```

3.3

```
PROGRAM sub(output);

CONST
   num1 = 47;
   num2 = 10;

BEGIN
   page(output);
   writeln(num1,' - ',num2,' = ',num1-num2)
END.
```

4.1

a = 20	b = 10	c = 2
d = 2	e = 60	f = 41

4.2
```
marks = 0..100;
vowels = ('a','e','i','o','u');
```

4.3
```
CONST
   maxi = 127;

TYPE
   int = -maxi..maxi;
```

4.6
```
simple(input,output);

VAR
   principal,intrate,noyears,interest : real;

BEGIN
   page(output);
   writeln;
   write('ENTER THE AMOUNT INVESTED -->');
   readln(principal);
   write('ENTER THE CURRENT INTEREST RATE -->');
   readln(intrate);
   write('ENTER THE NUMBER OF YEARS INVESTED -->');
   readln(noyears);
   interest := principal*noyears*(intrate/100.0);
   writeln('THE INTEREST IS ',interest)
END.
```

5.1
```
PROGRAM odd(input,output);

VAR
   number : integer;

BEGIN
   page(output);
   write('TYPE A NUMBER -->');
   readln(number);
   IF (number MOD 2)<>0 THEN
      writeln('THE NUMBER IS ODD')
END.
```

5.7
```
PROGRAM sqrroot(input,output);

VAR
   value,sqroot : real;
```

```
BEGIN
   page(output);
   write('ENTER A NUMBER -->');
   readln(value);
   IF value>0 THEN
      writeln('THE SQUARE ROOT IS ',sqrt(value))
   ELSE
      BEGIN
         writeln('YOU CANNOT TAKE THE SQUARE ROOTS');
         writeln('OF NEGATIVE NUMBERS')
      END
END.
```

6.1
```
PROGRAM stumarks(input,output);

CONST
   passmark = 35;

VAR
   nostudents : 0..maxint;
   nopass     : 0..maxint;
   nofail     : 0..maxint;
   mark       : 0..100;
   i          : integer;

BEGIN
   page(output);
   nopass := 0;
   nofail := 0;
   write('ENTER THE NUMBER OF STUDENTS -->');
   readln(nostudents);
   FOR i:=1 TO nostudents DO
      BEGIN
         write('ENTER MARK FOR STUDENT ',i,' -->');
         readln(mark);
         IF mark>=passmark THEN
             nopass := nopass+1
         ELSE
            nofail := nofail+1
      END;
   writeln('THERE WERE ',nopass,' PASSES');
   writeln('AND ',nofail,' FAILS')
END.
```

7.5 logtoanybase(number,base:REAL) : REAL;

```
BEGIN
   IF number <= 0.0 THEN
      BEGIN
        writeln('YOU CANNOT TAKE THE LOG OF ',number);
        logtoanybase := 0.0
      END
   ELSE
      IF base <= 0.0 THEN
         BEGIN
            writeln('THE BASE MUST BE POSITIVE, NOT ',base);
            logtoanybase := 0.0
         END
      ELSE
         logtoanybase := ln(number)/ln(base)
END;
```

Index